Valuable Friction

*How to Deliberately Stand Out in a
World Obsessed with Speed*

By Robert Rose

VALUABLE FRICTION

How to Deliberately Stand Out in a World Obsessed With Speed

ROBERT ROSE

Copyright © 2025 Robert Rose

All rights reserved. No part of this publication may be reproduced, distributed, or transmitted in any form or by any means, including photocopying, recording, or other electronic or mechanical methods, without the prior written permission of the publisher, except in the case of brief quotations embodied in critical reviews and certain other noncommercial uses permitted by copyright law.

ISBN: 979-8-9925206-8-2

Tilt Publishing
700 Park Offices Drive, Suite 250
Research Triangle, NC 27709

Table of Contents

Prologue: Resistance is Fertile 9

    Chapter 1: How Fast is Fast Enough? 13

    Chapter 2: Kill the Easy Button 25

    Chapter 3: Slower than the Algorithim 41

    Chapter 4: Deliberately Different 51

    Chapter 5: Creative Friction 61

    Chapter 6: Strategic Friction 73

    Chapter 7: Operational Friction 81

    Chapter 8: Relational Friction 95

    Chapter 9: The Practice of Friction 107

    Chapter 10: The Fewer-Better-Bolder Manifesto 121

Valuable Friction References 127

For Elizabeth-
You make me want to slow the world.
Your love is the stillness at the center,
the pause that makes any motion matter.

PROLOGUE

Resistance is Fertile

Spock: The Kobayashi Maru scenario frequently wreaks havoc on students and equipment. As I recall you took the test three times yourself. Your final solution was, shall we say, unique?
Kirk: It had the virtue of never having been tried.

—*Star Trek II: The Wrath of Khan*

Welcome. Take a minute. This book is going to help you use your time in a different way than you may be used to.

For one thing, it exposes the plain-vanilla result of the fast, easy seamlessness that's in vogue and explores the value that friction—resistance, strategic pause—can bring to your work and life.

Also, you don't need to read this book in order from "start" to "finish." You can start with any chapter and jump around to read what interests you. That's sort of the point.

Each chapter is a self-contained exploration of what I call Valuable Friction, which makes our work, our choices, and our relationships a little more intentional. Some are philosophical. Some are practical. All are designed to be read, revisited, and used. And they all lead to the more practical tools—and a bit of a community—that I have made available at ValuableFriction.com.

You can treat this book like a map, a mirror, or a meditation. Skip around. Re-read the bits that pull at something in your consciousness. Let them unfold in whatever order your attention chooses. What matters most is not where you begin, but that you begin noticing the moments in your work and life where friction adds value.

If you find guides helpful, here is a list of topics I cover:

1. **How Fast Is Fast Enough?**

   Questioning the cult of speed before it flattens everything

   Speed has become the unquestioned default of modern life—praised as progress, pursued as purpose. But when we treat faster as better without asking why, we lose the friction that gives weight to our choices, depth to our work, and shape to our lives.

2. **Kill the Easy Button**

   Surfing the Friction Balance Curve before seamless turns soulless

   Convenience, when unexamined, can dull meaning and differentiation—so we must find the balance where friction deepens value instead of erasing it.

3. **Slower than the Algorithm**

   Outsmarting instant answers with deliberation

   This chapter challenges the rush to embrace the quick, shiny solution and instead invites a deliberate pause—leaning into cognitive friction to uncover richer insights. By slowing down—questioning assumptions, letting ideas marinate, and probing beneath the surface—we reveal more original, human-centered solutions than any snap judgment can deliver.

4. **Deliberately Different**

   The four frictions that keep your work from melting into meh

   Valuable Friction, designed to help you stand out, can be seen through four forms—creative, strategic, operational, and relational. Each enriches experience and differentiates work.

5. **Creative Friction**

   Constraints, tension, and the alchemy of turning limits into lightning

   Constraints and tension can spark originality, making friction essential to authentic and memorable creative work.

6. **Strategic Friction**

   Pauses, pushback, and the decision-making friction that differentiates

   Deliberate pauses and tension in decision-making create better strategy by surfacing clarity, risk, and alignment before action.

7. **Operational Friction**

   Rhythms and rituals that make how you work impossible to copy

   Rituals, rhythms, and structured checkpoints prevent chaos and keep quality and alignment intact as teams move quickly.

8. **Relational Friction**

   Slow conversations that outlast any scroll

   Trust and psychological safety grow when teams hold emotional tension with care—turning feedback, conflict, and vulnerability into connection.

9. **The Practice of Friction**

   Turning theory into muscle memory, one intention at a time

   Using friction well requires a mindset shift and a practice of noticing, evaluating, and designing resistance that enhances trust, clarity, and connection.

10. **The Fewer–Better–Bolder Manifesto**

    Standing apart by choosing less, deciding better, and acting louder

    By focusing on a handful of high-leverage actions, making more thoughtful decisions, and embracing bold experimentation, you turn constraints into catalysts for breakthrough ideas—and build the confidence to lead rather than follow.

You can read this book as a field guide. A provocation. A quiet rebellion against the cult of seamlessness. You don't need permission to start.

But if you're looking for a sign, this is it.

CHAPTER ONE

How Fast is Fast Enough?

Questioning the Cult of Speed before it Flattens Everything

> *"Slow down, you're doin' fine.*
> *You can't be everything you wanna be before your time."*
>
> —Billy Joel, "Vienna"

We are living in extraordinary times. Opportunities abound to reshape how people think, work, and connect with the world. Yet the pressure to *do*—to be busy, to execute, to keep moving—is relentless. Too few of us take a moment to "waste" time thinking. We leap right to the doing.

A friend of mine recently shared a story about a mentor who gave him some counterintuitive advice on time management: "Your inability to waste minutes and hours is the reason you'll end up wasting months and years."

I love that.

It echoes a quote often attributed to psychologist Amos Tversky: "The secret to doing good research is always to be a little underemployed. You waste years by not being able to waste hours."

But I prefer my friend's version. It shifts the emphasis from the external pressure of busyness to an internal choice. The decision *not* to fill every moment. The courage to "waste time", on purpose.

Without this, we're missing something essential: the nourishing experiences that come from doing difficult work. The kind of work shaped by what I call "Valuable Friction".

So, what does Valuable Friction mean?

Let's stop for a moment and think about it.

The Medium, the Message, and the Mistake

Over the last quarter century, we've ridden wave after wave of technological transformation—a whirlwind of acceleration:

- In the last years of the 20th century and early in the 21st, broadband internet and search engines redefined how we find information.
- In the 2000s and 2010s, e-commerce platforms and on-demand services redefined how we buy, sell, and move goods—turning convenience into a business model.
- Beginning in the early 2000s, social media platforms introduced the infinite scroll and rewrote how we engage with our families, friends, customers, and communities.
- Beginning in 2007, mobile computing put the internet in our pockets, disrupting the frequency and context for connection, content creation, and consumption.
- In the 2010s, data and algorithms began to quietly curate our digital lives, turning personalization into prediction and nudging us to want things before we knew we wanted them.

And now, generative AI is turning the world of creativity upside down, changing not just the speed of expression but the very nature of creative labor itself.

We Built the Tools. Then the Tools Built Us.

You've probably heard the quote—often misattributed to philosopher and author Marshall McLuhan—"We shape our tools, and then our tools shape us." That phrase was actually coined by his friend and collaborator Father John Culkin, and it described McLuhan's point of view remarkably well.[1] But it's helpful here because it clarifies McLuhan's more cryptic, and more famous, phrase: *The medium is the message.*

When we create any new medium—electricity, the internet, social media, AI—the initial shape of the innovation is ours. But the long-term effects—the message—are what that tool does to us. And there's no doubt that the medium of the last 25 years has been grounded upon one thing: speed.

- We don't memorize; we Google. It's faster.
- We don't call; we post or message. It's more efficient.
- We don't browse; we compare. It's optimized.
- We don't decide; we're nudged. It's frictionless.

And soon, we may not decide to purchase products at all, as our agents negotiate with other agents on our behalf, given pre-determined rules we have established.

Wait a minute! What does this have to do with friction? And, specifically, how does this relate to standing out in the world?

Let's begin with the first question. If the rallying cry of the last two decades has been agility plus convenience, the result is plain: we now treat *speed* as the master metric of business, creativity, and our culture.

Our culture now celebrates mantras like:

- Move fast and break things
- Fail fast
- Done is better than perfect
- Build the plane while flying it
- Speed is a feature

From students to CEOs, velocity has become shorthand for value. We measure ourselves in throughput, celebrate quick pivots, and make *faster* the goal—often without knowing what we're racing toward.

So I came to a working hypothesis: Maybe speed isn't a synonym for progress at all. Maybe it's a drug: effective in small doses, disastrous in binges, and—crucially—renders us incapable of distinguishing between momentum and meaning. If that's true, then the question isn't "How do we go faster?" but "How fast is fast enough to stay alive without blurring the destination?"

Which brings me to the follow-up question: If we *can* pinpoint how fast is fast enough, what advantage does that unlock?

Why Standing Out Now Matters More than Ever

Scroll any feed for sixty seconds and you'll witness a paradox: an infinite torrent of content that somehow feels monotonous. When friction disappears from creation and distribution, everything and everybody starts to look, sound, and think alike. Originality flattens into memes; conviction dissolves into a perceived consensus.

We do try. We try words, images, logos, self-help books, tips, tricks. But none of it seems to work. It's all so easily copied or just feels temporary. And yes, I do get the irony of those last two sentences. But, my goal here is not to provide easy answers for you, as much as it is to simply ask you to wrestle with some questions.

This flattening of originality raised for me a second, equally pressing hypothesis: In an age of effortless broadcast, the scarcest resource is no longer information—it's our unique selves. Deciding differently, operating differently, and relating differently may soon be the *only* durable competitive advantage left. Standing out isn't a marketing slogan; it's a modern survival strategy.

But let's not take both of those ideas at face value. Let's wrestle with them a bit more.

And that circles us back to the question I keep asking:

How Fast is Fast Enough?

It's a question that tends to settle into a room rather than interrupt it. I ask it often in strategy meetings or workshops, when someone says, "We need to move faster." Almost always, the room gets quiet. Not in resistance—more like in recognition. As if we've all been racing for a long time without ever agreeing on where the finish line is, much less on how quickly we need to reach it.

Speed became the goal in and of itself. More output, faster. More channels, all at once. More convenience. More now.

We optimized everything for velocity—not just in how we work but in how we learn, communicate, consume, and even create. Speed didn't just shape our systems. It started shaping our expectations, our habits, and our sense of what progress looks like.

But what have we lost in the process?

Speed, unchecked, flattens things. It can make everything feel urgent but nothing feel meaningful. When all friction is removed, every delay is smoothed out, and every hesitation designed away, what's left is often something unmemorable. Or worse, untrustworthy.

This question—*how fast is fast enough?*—isn't entirely new. Carl Honoré helped spark the Slow Movement over twenty years ago by challenging our addiction to speed. His point wasn't that fast is bad but that the right speed is intentional. In his 2004 book, *In Praise of Slowness: Challenging the Cult of Speed*, he said: "The secret is balance: instead of doing everything faster, do everything at the right speed. Sometimes fast. Sometimes slow. Sometimes in between."[2]

Others have taken up that thread. In his 2018 essay "The Tyranny of Convenience", Tim Wu warned that unexamined convenience "with its promise of smooth, effortless efficiency, threatens to erase the sort of struggles and challenges that help give meaning to life."[3] And researcher Renée Gosline has argued that even in digital design, we shouldn't eliminate all friction. In her 2022 *Harvard Business Review* article, "Why AI Customer Journeys Need More Friction," Gosline challenges the prevailing notion that all friction in user experiences should be eliminated. She argues that while reducing unnecessary obstacles is beneficial, introducing deliberate, well-designed friction can enhance user trust and decision-making. For example, the confirmation screen before you delete a file—"are you sure?"—helps to slow you down and protect you. She argues that not all friction is a "pain point," saying, "When it comes to the adoption of AI and machine learning, 'frictionless' strategies can also lead to harm, from privacy and surveillance concerns to algorithms' capacity to reflect and amplify bias."[4]

So, Why the Word "Friction"?

Friction, in its simplest form, is resistance. A bit of drag. The thing that slows the wheel or stops the slide. And for most of our modern lives, we've been taught that it's a problem to solve. So why choose this word when something like "braking," "thoughtfulness," or "intentionality" might sound gentler?

For me, it's because *friction* names the force we've been trained to eliminate. It reminds us that resistance isn't always an obstacle; sometimes it's a signal. A teacher. A boundary. A shaping pressure. It's what gives us traction. What makes things real.

Friction is also the point of contact between momentum and meaning. And in the physical world, that means it's not just a brake—it also creates heat, and then a *spark*.

That's the kind of friction we need more of.

Friction, when it's intentional, demands something of us—attention, presence, patience—and in doing so, it deepens our connection to what we're engaging with: a decision, a product, a person, a story.

Thus, the theme of this book is friction—not as a flaw to eliminate, but as a way of operating. Because the truth is that friction shows up wherever different forces, speeds, or needs collide. And those collisions don't have to just slow us down—they can shape what lasts.

A Thought I had in 1999 that I'm Just Now Understanding

Not many books feel more relevant two decades after their publication than they did when they first came out. But *The Clock of the Long Now* does. Published in 1999, it wasn't just a book about a 10,000-year timepiece—it was a guide to cultivating long-term thinking in an age obsessed with immediacy. Author Stewart Brand used the design of the clock as a metaphor for something bigger: How do we make long-term thinking automatic and common instead of difficult and rare?

He argued that to face an accelerating future, we need continuity, discipline, and room to imagine the improbable. It was both a philosophical treatise and a practical manifesto—a blend of future tech and timeless wisdom that, in hindsight, feels like required reading we mostly skipped as a culture.

I first read *The Clock of the Long Now* back in 1999, just as we were all collectively losing our minds over Y2K and wondering if AltaVista or Ask Jeeves was going to win the search engine wars. Amid all that techno-optimism (and panic), Brand's ideas landed like a glass of cold water—and a bit of a gut punch.

In particular, his concept of Pace Layering stuck with me. I didn't fully grasp it at the time, but that didn't stop me from quoting it like I did. I've been thinking about this model for 25 years. And if I'm honest, it's only now—after two decades of watching technology outrun our ability to process it—that I feel like I'm finally starting to understand what Brand was trying to warn us about.

The model lays out six layers of civilization, each operating at its own speed:

- **Fashion**—Changes rapidly (months to years)
- **Commerce**—Driven by markets and cycles (1–10 years)
- **Infrastructure**—Systems like transportation and utilities (10–100 years)
- **Governance**—Laws and institutions (25–100 years)
- **Culture**—Norms and traditions (hundreds of years)
- **Nature**—The slowest of all (geological time)

The genius of this framework is in its balance. Fast layers take risks and drive change. Slow layers provide stability and memory. Each layer depends on the ones below to hold it up—and gently pressures the ones above to evolve.

"Fast learns, slow remembers." —Stewart Brand

It's a model that values tension. A model that sees friction not as a flaw, but as a feature.

Why Friction Belongs at the Boundaries

This brings me back to *Valuable Friction*, a term you may think sounds like something overheard at a Silicon Valley offsite, maybe sandwiched between "radical candor" and "moonshot mindset." Yeah, I get it. But I promise that it's more grounded than it sounds.

Friction lives in the boundaries between Brand's layers. It shows up where fast meets slow—where the next big thing collides with the realities of infrastructure, policy, or culture. It's the force that makes us pause. Reconsider. Adapt. Occasionally scream into a pillow.

In other words—and this is the important part—*Valuable Friction is not about moving faster or slower. It's about using the difference between those tempos to your advantage.* To set yourself apart from those stuck in the layer above or below. To operate at the boundary where insight, influence, and originality live.

Everyone in the reality we all share is afforded the same amount of time in a minute, a day, or a year. But Valuable Friction is how we use time differently than the world around us.

And that might be the most valuable thing of all.

In a world optimized for urgency, *friction is how we make room for intention.*

We feel it when a handwritten note means more than a text. When taking that long walk lingers in memory more than the fast ride. When a story unfolds slowly and stays with us rather than being over in a binge-watch. Friction, in those cases, isn't the enemy. It's the reason the experience mattered.

In that sense, Valuable Friction is a kind of design principle—not just for systems and products, but for how we work, create, and live. It's the purposeful decision *not* to eliminate every difficulty but instead to leave just enough resistance in the process to keep it honest. To make it real.

Of course, not all friction is valuable. Some is just poor design or needless bureaucracy. But the answer isn't to remove all of it. It's to discern. To ask where ease is helpful—and where effort creates meaning.

That brings us to the second hypothesis: that differentiating ourselves may be our best chance at competitive advantage. Let's look at the benefit of Valuable Friction—or rather, why we should care about practicing it.

Why Different Matters

In a swipe-to-copy world—where a classmate can ChatGPT-clone your essay by dawn and your family can Amazon Prime the same meal kit as every other household—content isn't scarce; choices are. A graduate's résumé may list the usual bullets but the candidate who slows down long enough to show *how* they framed the problem, iterated the draft, and invited critique instantly rises above the stack. That is, of course, assuming that the reviewer is also practicing a bit of Valuable Friction themselves.

A household deciding to ditch "device-distracted dinners" for tech-free tacos makes a similarly rare move: they build a little friction into the evening so real conversation can surface. Or that founder who resists the hurry to ship a "minimum viable clone" and instead labors over a sturdier problem statement, a tighter user interview loop, or a more intentional culture code plants a flag that no "vibe coder" can steal. In all of these cases, the edge no algorithm can counterfeit is how *you* steer—the deliberate pauses, honest detours, and slow questions that expose your true outline.

That's why purposeful drag matters. *Your choice of friction reveals YOU.* The split-second you wrestle with a decision, rough draft something twice, or invite pushback, you leave fingerprints no one can Ctrl-C. Anyone can replicate information; nobody can replicate the miles you logged thinking it through.

So, differentiation migrates upstream from deliverables to disciplines. It shows up in:

- **The way you create** (choosing constraints over shortcuts)
- **The way you strategize** (building pause points instead of knee-jerk pivots)
- **The way you operate** (favoring rituals that build craft over hacks that burn it)
- **The way you relate** (allowing tension so trust has room to grow)

These are the four motions you can practice in this book—creative, strategic, operational, and relational. Each one layers intentional resistance into everyday life, so when your work or presence hits the public feed, it carries fingerprints, not factory gloss. Because what the world ultimately notices isn't the speed of your output; it's the unmistakable outline of someone who chose to move fewer, faster, bolder—on purpose.

I don't know about you, but after 25 years of rushing through everything, I think I'm finally ready to take this seriously.

CHAPTER 2

Kill the Easy Button

Surfing the Friction Balance Curve
before Seamless turns Soulless

*"You can't always get what you want...
But if you try sometimes, you might find...
You get what you need."*

—The Rolling Stones, "You Can't Always Get What You Want"

When I was a teenager in Dallas, my cheap stereo FM radio was my lifeline to something bigger. Every Sunday night I'd tune into Jim Ladd's *Innerview*, which was broadcast nationally from Los Angeles but felt like it was beamed straight into my bedroom. Jim was amazing. Fun side note: Jim is who Tom Petty's song "The Last DJ" is about.[5] Jim didn't just spin records—he told stories. He'd sit down with legends like Phil Collins and talk, *really* talk. About the meaning behind the music. About the weird twists of their lives. About the creative process. Then, he'd play the songs between the stories.

That was my moment.

I'd sit cross-legged on my bedroom floor, finger hovering above the "Record" button, waiting and praying that I'd hit it fast enough when "The Lamb Lies

Down on Broadway" started. Sometimes I'd nail it. Sometimes I'd get half a sentence from Jim right in the middle of the intro. That became part of the charm. Every mixtape had a few scars—warped transitions, half-faded outros, and whatever static the Texas airwaves delivered that night.

But here's the thing: those tapes meant something. Every track had to be earned. You had to wait. You had to listen. You had to *care*. I once spent two hours waiting just to catch "Sara" by Fleetwood Mac at the perfect moment. Why? To impress a girl. (Give me a break; I was 13.)

Fast forward to now, and I can literally whisper a lyric into my phone and hear it in two seconds. Any song. Any version. Any time. And you know what? It just doesn't land the same.

Music used to be something I pursued. Now, it just *arrives*. Flawless. Instant. Frictionless.

Before you tell me I'm an old man yelling at clouds, it turns out there's science behind that feeling. Behavioral economists and consumer psychologists have long studied the relationship between effort and value. One key finding: The more we work for something, the more we tend to treasure it. Scarcity and difficulty don't just make things harder—they tend to make them matter.

In *Decoded: The Science Behind Why We Buy*, author Phil Barden discusses how value is perceived not just rationally but through emotional and contextual clues—including effort, availability, and motivation.[6] When you have every song, every movie, and every product at your fingertips, the individual pieces lose their shine. There's no hunt, no waiting, no selection ritual. Just … consumption.

The same goes for ideas. Experiences. Even relationships.

Convenience flattens the terrain. What used to feel like magic becomes background noise. What once felt like a curated mixtape becomes a shuffled algorithm.

Or, as author Clay Shirky put it in a 2010 keynote: "Abundance breaks more things than scarcity. Society knows how to react to scarcity."[7]

Let's talk about why that matters.

The Dark Side of Convenience

We tend to talk about convenience as if it were an unquestioned good. Who wouldn't want things to be easier? Faster? Closer to effortless?

And yet, convenience has a strange side effect. Over time, it changes our expectations—not just of services or products, but of ourselves. What once felt like a helpful improvement becomes a baseline requirement. What used to feel special becomes mundane.

This is the dark side of convenience: it creates smoother surfaces, but often at the cost of texture, substance, or meaning. It promises to save time, but often fills that saved time with more noise, not more life.

We see it everywhere: the streaming service that skips credits before we've even decided if we liked what we watched. The countdown to "next episode" that has us scrambling for the remote so we can navigate away before the next one accidentally starts. The email tool that finishes our sentences or writes the entire email. The smart fridge that restocks itself.

The idea that we can live, create, and relate with minimal friction has become aspirational—maybe even moral. As if ease were always a virtue.

But what if convenience, when left unexamined, narrows our lives instead of enriching them? What if it lowers the stakes of our choices, dulls our attention, and trains us to overlook the very effort that gives something value?

Convenience isn't wrong, but it's not neutral. And it's certainly not free.

Helpful Ease vs. Harmful Automation

There is, of course, a kind of ease that feels like a gift. It makes you feel as if all is right with the world.

- The well-designed door handle.
- The intuitive form that doesn't make you guess.
- The coffee machine that remembers your favorite brew.

Good design—human-centered design—removes unnecessary obstacles. It anticipates needs. It respects your time, your energy, and your focus. These moments of helpful ease don't strip away meaning. They make space for it.

And this is where things get a bit complicated.

You see, we also live in a culture that often confuses struggle with virtue. We're taught that the hard way is the right way. That value lies in sacrifice. That if something isn't difficult, it isn't worthwhile.

In creative work, we mythologize the tortured artist. In learning, we mistake confusion about the lesson for depth of teaching. In entrepreneurship, we glorify burnout as a badge of honor. Ease, in this sense, becomes an "enemy" to perceived value.

In other words, we believe that with more struggle comes more meaning or value. But we also believe that things should be as easy as possible.

But not all ease is helpful. And not all struggle is meaningful.

The enemy is the disengagement that can come from *harmful* ease, or automation. This removes friction—the kind that sharpens us, makes us better, teaches us something.

In creative work, that friction is the blank page, the rough draft, the unexpected idea. In learning, it's the pause to reflect, the question that doesn't have a tidy answer. In leadership, it's the tension of being okay with not knowing, of listening longer than is comfortable, of allowing for competing truths without judgment. These are not inefficiencies to be optimized away. They are the points of contact where meaning is made.

The difference between helpful ease and harmful automation is subtle. Take these examples:

- A default setting you never question.

- An algorithm that tells you what to like.
- An AI that finishes your sentence before you've even figured out what you're trying to say.

At first, these systems feel smart. They anticipate. They accelerate. They reduce the burden.

But slowly, they start making choices for us. And we stop noticing that we've stopped choosing.

We begin to confuse the ease of something with its value. And in doing so, we give away the essential human work of creative tension: discernment, originality, curiosity, care.

Behavioral economists Richard Thaler and Cass Sunstein introduced the concept of the "nudge" in their book *Nudge: Improving Decisions About Health, Wealth, and Happiness*.[8] They suggest a way to design choices that "nudge" people into making better decisions without removing their freedom. That is helpful ease. But they also later named a shadow version of this idea: sludge. Sludge is friction that obstructs rather than guides. An example would be a default workflow that makes it easier to accept the status quo than to think critically about an alternative. Even good automation can become sludge if it replaces engagement with efficiency. And sometimes that difference is really in the eye of the beholder:

For example, Netflix introduced the "Skip Intro" button for its series in 2017. They had noticed that around 15% of viewers were fast-forwarding through the first five minutes of programming. From that, they concluded audiences wanted a way to bypass opening credits altogether.[9]

Now, you might look at that number and say, "Well, that means 85% weren't skipping the intro." And that's true. But Netflix saw an opportunity to *nudge* people with a new feature—without taking away the freedom to experience the intro if they chose.

So why, in 2025, are creators still producing lush theme songs and intricate opening sequences? Because they believe these elements are essential to the artistic experience of a show. Opening credits set the tone. They credit the cast and crew. They establish a brand. And perhaps most importantly, they create a moment of connection and anticipation—a small, intentional pause that helps deepen our emotional connection to the story.

But in the name of speed and efficiency, Netflix decided that skipping that moment should be a choice. So is that a nudge? Or is it sludge? On the surface, it seems like a nudge—after all, it gives users control. But we might also ask whether, in a culture obsessed with speed, we've been trained to crave that convenience. And if we're always choosing to skip ahead, are we actually better off? Did we have a more valuable experience?

In a wonderful 2022 episode of the *Still Processing* podcast, Wesley Morris and Hanif Abdurraqib debate the value of the "Skip Intro" button. They suggest that theme songs and opening credits aren't just aesthetic flair. With repetition, they become something deeper—personal soundtracks. Emotional muscle memory. They don't just evoke the show; they evoke a time, a feeling, even a version of ourselves.[10]

I really identify with that. I can still sing the theme song to *Star Trek* or *The Bugs Bunny Show*, and immediately be transported to the best memories of my childhood. Those intros anchored me in the best version of myself. I would never have skipped them—even if I could. They signaled to my child brain that good stuff was coming.

Today, what was once a moment of forced friction—"good stuff is coming"—has become "here's your option to get to the good stuff faster." I understand it's a choice, and that makes it a feature. But I'm not convinced we're better off for it.

All I'm suggesting is this: take a moment to ask yourself, *"am I really better off skipping the intro?"*

Because once we stop noticing the difference, we stop participating in the process altogether.

And that is when we lose not just our edge, but our agency. We begin to look like everyone else, saying the exact same things in the exact same way.

How Convenience Shapes Habits and Decisions

Convenience, like water, follows the path of least resistance. And over time, we do too.

What begins as a helpful shortcut quietly becomes a default. A habit. A norm. We stop choosing and start expecting. Eventually, we forget there was ever another way.

That's the quiet power of frictionless design: it doesn't just save time. It shapes attention. It trains preference. It conditions us to seek the smoothest path—not because it's better, but because it's faster and demands less of us.

We don't just learn to enjoy ease. We start to expect it. And once we do, its absence begins to feel like a problem.

This is the deeper risk: convenience doesn't only remove effort—it erodes our tolerance for effort. And when that happens, we become less patient with ambiguity, less curious in the face of complexity, less willing to stay in the tension that creativity, learning, or leadership often require.

Think about how we learn. Research shows that small, intentional obstacles—what psychologists call *desirable difficulties*[11]—can actually improve retention and mastery. But we still reach for the easy read, the tidy summary, the skip-intro button. Not because it serves us better but because it's more comfortable in the moment.

Or think about food. A microwave meal is frictionless, but also forgettable. A home-cooked dish takes more time and focus—maybe even a few mistakes. But those steps are part of the memory. Part of the meaning. The ritual matters, even when the result is imperfect.

And then there are our digital routines. We swipe, scroll, respond—without deciding to. These aren't instincts. They're trained responses. Learned behaviors. And convenience is what taught them to us.

The problem isn't speed. It's the flattening—the smoothing—of experience. When everything arrives without friction, nothing feels worth the effort.

The playlist we handcrafted feels the same as the one the algorithm made. The article we searched for sits beside a headline we never wanted.

To be clear, this isn't a call to reject convenience. We don't need to make everything harder just to prove we care. But we do need to notice what we lose when we stop noticing altogether. A little friction—a pause, a prompt, a pattern that resists autopilot—can restore intention. It's the gap between reacting and responding. Between letting the system steer us and deciding where we actually want to go.

In a culture that prizes speed and simplification, effort can feel subversive. But it's also what makes something ours.

The Cost of Trust, Satisfaction, and Yes, Differentiation

One of the great ironies of a frictionless world is this: many of the moments we cherish—those that feel most meaningful—weren't necessarily difficult. But they did require something…else. That "something else" might be time, attention, or simply presence. In other words, don't forget that as much as we try to engineer inconvenience out of our own life—we appreciate it when it exists on our behalf.

Even if the experience came easily, if we found it exceptional it's probably because it felt like the person behind it made a deliberate choice not to rush. It wasn't difficult by default—but it wasn't careless either. Not because it had to be hard but because it *deserved* to be meaningful. For example, think of any product you purchase from Apple. That little white ribbon you tug gives you exactly the right amount of resistance—fast enough that you don't get bored, slow enough that you definitely value the contents even more.

But here's the thing. As participants in those experiences, we can often misread that "something else" as struggle. And so, because we value it, we try to mirror it—by performing or signaling struggle in return.

I touched on this earlier. We live in a culture that tends to conflate struggle with significance. It's the unspoken belief that difficulty equals depth. The performance of hardship as a kind of social currency.

Think about how often we reach for that instinct when we're trying to signal value to someone:

- Someone asks how your flight to the conference was and you sigh: "It was brutal." It actually wasn't that hard, but we believe they'll appreciate our presence more if they think we suffered to get there.
- Someone compliments the work we delivered and, instead of saying "It came together quickly," we recount every obstacle—because we think the work will seem more impressive if it *seemed harder to achieve.*

We do this reflexively—not to deceive, but to try and prove value through demonstrating effort. As if the only way to earn someone's appreciation is to demonstrate that we suffered to be there.

Psychologists call this effort justification—the tendency to overvalue something because it was hard to get. But in practice, we use it less to convince ourselves and more to convince each other. To signal worth, effort, or legitimacy through a story of struggle.

But what if we didn't have to do that? What if introducing some friction into those interactions could balance the idea of perceived value and struggle? What if our signal of care didn't have to be wrapped in the easier, faster narrative of pain?

Imagine a different kind of answer. Someone asks how your trip was and you say: "The flight was wonderful—surprisingly smooth—and it gave me a moment to feel grateful I could be here." Or a friend we haven't seen in a while asks how we've been and we're actually doing really well. Instead of focusing on some recent difficulty or downshifting to "pretty good" or "fine" to avoid sounding out of touch, we pause, step into the friction, and offer something more honest: "I'm actually doing fantastic—and I'd love to hear how *you're* doing."

That small shift is friction. Not because it's hard to say, but because it resists the instinct to take the friction out of the interaction and sand down our emotion (whatever it may be). It trusts that presence doesn't have to be symmetrical to be meaningful, and that you don't have to take the easiest way out to avoid something that might, at first, feel a bit awkward.

This level of friction plays an enormous role in how we begin to establish deeper levels of trust, whether it's with our colleagues, our boss, our customers, or even our friends.

Ultimately, convenience can be useful—but it can also be flattening. When every experience you create is designed to be easy (positively or negatively), it becomes harder to distinguish one from the next. Everything begins to feel the same. And sameness makes it harder for anything to feel trustworthy or worth remembering.

This is where differentiation quietly erodes. When a product, service, or message asks nothing of us—no thought, no pause, no presence—it rarely leaves a mark. But the ones that do—the ones we remember—often ask just enough. Think of the Apple packaging, or…

- The boss who writes the big task-filled email on Sunday but waits until Monday to send it, because timing is part of the care.
- The collaborator who insists on a kickoff call—not because it's required, but because it makes the work feel shared from the start.
- The team that opens their retreat with ten minutes of silence—not because it's efficient, but because it invites everyone to focus their attention.
- The client who says "Take your time" and means it—not to slow you down, but to make space for better thinking.

This kind of caring—whether it required effort or not—is what makes a difference. That's the deeper cost of unchecked convenience. Not that it makes things too easy—but that it makes them less distinct.

And in a world where trust is fragile, attention is fleeting, and meaning is often manufactured, that's a cost too high to ignore.

The Friction Balance Curve

When we step back and look at all of this—the difference between helpful and harmful automation, the way convenience reshapes our habits, and the quiet toll it can take on trust and differentiation—a pattern begins to emerge.

The problem isn't drag. And it isn't ease.

The real challenge is knowing *how much* of either belongs in any given moment.

Sometimes a little friction makes the experience. Sometimes it breaks it.

There is an old quote by statistician George Box that says, "All models are wrong, but some are useful." It means that statistical models will always fall short of the complexities of reality—but if used as an exercise they can still provide helpful insight. Valuable Friction, indeed.

This is absolutely true of my Friction Balance Curve model. It's not meant to be a perfect reflection of reality, nor is it meant to be a checklist for every interaction you'll have. Yeah, don't pull this out when you arrive for lunch with that wonderful friend—that's unhelpful friction.

But hopefully it can be a useful tool for you to begin a practice. It's not a formula to solve but a lens to look through. A way to examine the relationship between how much friction something asks of us and how much engagement, meaning, or memory it creates in return.

In a world that constantly optimizes for ease, this curve invites us to think a little differently. To ask: *Is this friction getting in the way—or is it doing something valuable?*

How the Curve Works

The Friction Balance Curve maps the relationship between friction and engagement/value in any task, experience, or interaction. So, the Y axis is the spectrum between meaningful value and meaninglessness. The X axis represents the balance of Friction from Excessive Ease to Unhelpful Friction.

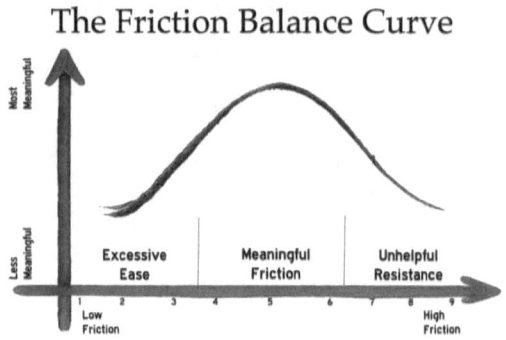

- On the left side is excessive ease—interactions that are so effortless they feel disposable. There's no pause, no thought, no memory made.
- On the right is unhelpful friction—effort that confuses, frustrates, or slows us down without purpose.
- At the peak of a curved line, we find Valuable Friction—just enough resistance to signal care, build trust, and make something feel worth it.

You don't need to quantify it. You just need to notice two things:

- How much effort does this ask for? (*Level of Effort*) Maybe choose a number from one to ten to represent the effort and plot it along the Friction axis.

- How much emotional or experiential value does it create? (*Meaning Made*) Again, choose a number from one to ten to represent the effort and plot it along the Meaning axis.

A small shift in friction—either more or less—might be what moves a task, experience, or interaction from forgettable to memorable.

Using the Curve to Evaluate Existing Experiences

Let's ground the model with two real-world examples and how it might differentiate your experience.

Example 1: You want to create a new newsletter signup on your website

- **Excessive Ease**: A single-field form with no context. You enter your email, hit submit, and that's it. It's fast—but forgettable. It feels generic.
- **Meaningful Friction**: A second field asks, "Why do you want to hear from us?", offers a short sentence about what the newsletter stands for, or simply asks for some fun or even completely random question ("What's your favorite cat?). Now you've invited reflection. You've created a signal. You've given the reader a role to play to begin a relationship.
- **Unhelpful Friction**: A multi-step signup process with login creation, email verification, and unnecessary data capture. Now you've added weight with no value.

Example 2: A one-on-one check-in with your employee

- **Excessive Ease**: The meeting opens with "Everything good?" The reply is a polite nod. Nothing real is exchanged.
- **Meaningful Friction**: You start with a shared ritual: "What's one thing you've been sitting with this week but have made no decision

about?" It's small, but it creates a shift. It says, "We're here for more than surface updates."

- **Unhelpful Friction**: You overload the check-in with a rigid form, excessive prep work, or unclear purpose. The space feels more performative than supportive.

These examples show how tuning friction—just slightly—can make something more distinct and more meaningful.

A Simple Diagnostic for Finding the Sweet Spot

Try these reflection questions to get a sense of where a task, moment, or system might land on the curve:

1. **How much friction does this experience currently have?**
   - It's so easy it feels like it doesn't matter
   - It's just challenging enough to feel personal or intentional
   - It's confusing, slow, or off-putting
2. **How meaningful or memorable is it to the person involved?**
   - They forget it immediately
   - They feel seen, considered, or engaged
   - They feel annoyed, exhausted, or disengaged

Where your answers land is likely where the experience sits on the curve.

Want more examples and deeper questions? You'll find additional friction diagnostics at www.valuablefriction.com.

Using the Curve as a Design Decision Filter

Sometimes the best use of the Curve isn't to evaluate what already exists—it's to help you decide what to build. So you can also use it as a design tool by asking this question:

"If we add this extra step, does it move us into unhelpful friction? Or is it a moment that could create meaning?"

The Curve becomes a conversation starter. A guide for testing intention.

This design-facing use case—and templates for applying it across teams—can also be found at www.valuablefriction.com.

Because when you get friction right, you don't just create better experiences. You create things that stay with people.

A Gentle Return to Effort

Convenience, when thoughtfully applied, can be a gift. But when it becomes the default value—the thing we prize above all else—it begins to shape us in ways we didn't actively choose. It flattens the terrain. It narrows our attention. It teaches us to mistake ease for meaning and speed for success. It makes us part of everything else.

This doesn't mean we need to reject technology or abandon the tools that make modern life possible. It simply means we need to reclaim our relationship with effort—not as something to be avoided, but as something that can anchor us.

Convenience is a current. Left unexamined, it carries us without asking where we want to go. But Valuable Friction—deliberate, meaningful, human—gives us something to push against. It helps us steer. It gives shape to our attention and purpose to our motion.

CHAPTER 3

Slower than the Algorithim

Outsmarting Instant Answers with Deliberation

"Did you exchange a walk-on part in the war for a lead role in a cage?"

—*Pink Floyd, "Wish You Were Here"*

There was a time when knowing something meant spending time with it—literally.

In the Middle Ages, monastic communities played a critical role in preserving and transmitting knowledge, especially after the fall of the Roman Empire. Monks spent their lives hand-copying manuscripts—page by page, line by line—creating illuminating texts that included not only Christian theology but also the works of ancient Greece and Rome. Each page represented hours of focused labor, infused with care and reverence.

But the monasteries weren't just preserving knowledge. They were shaping people. Through slow, deliberate study and reflection, monks didn't simply learn what to believe—they came to understand *why*. This wasn't just the transfer of content. It was the formation of character. The effort to know was inseparable from the conviction that followed.

Over time, those monastic schools evolved into universities such as Oxford, Cambridge, and others. And from those slow, candle-lit acts of learning came a generation of thinkers, teachers, and leaders who could not only hold knowledge but *stand inside it*.

I think about that kind of knowing when I reflect on one of my first jobs in marketing. It was the 1990s, and I was working at Showtime Networks. My first assignment wasn't glamorous. I was asked to read through the entire programming slate—every show the network had, every proposal in development, every review we had on file—and organize it. Summarize it. Categorize it. Turn it into usable language that our marketing team could share with cable company operators.

Let me be clear—while the monks were learning through Plato, Aristotle, and the poets Virgil and Horace, I was learning through the illustrious works of Mrs. Piggle-Wiggle, Red Shoe Diaries, and Saturday Night Boxing.

Wisdom it was not. And it took weeks. There was no shortcut. No search bar. No AI assistant to condense it into tidy bullets. It was just me, a stack of books, a legal pad, and a mountain of context.

But here's the thing: by the time I was finished, I didn't just know the programming—I *understood* it. I could talk about it. Defend it. Suggest future shows we should pursue (not that they ever asked me). Spot gaps in our lineup. My conviction didn't come from how much I'd memorized; it came from knowing why I knew it. Because I'd done the work.

That experience didn't just teach me about my job—it taught me something that I could use in my career.

The Meaning of Leadership

Thirty years on from my adventures at Showtime, I meet regularly with a group of seasoned professionals to explore big ideas, emerging trends, and how we might anticipate what's coming next in the business world.

The insights and learning from these meetings are invaluable. But the real magic isn't in the ideas. It's in the shared stories, the deep relationships, and the friendships that have grown over the years.

Our facilitator likes to say, "It's not networking; it's community-ing." And, honestly, that's what makes these discussions different. They're not just about tossing around theories—they're about challenging each other, sharpening perspectives, and realizing that the future might be much weirder than we thought.

At one of these events, we took on a big and modern question that led to some fascinating discussions: "How will AI reshape what it means to be a leader?"

We explored this from every angle: political leadership, corporate leadership, and even leadership within small groups and communities. But the common, implicit theme was around how one differentiates oneself to become a leader in the modern world of AI.

We started with a question: What happens when everyone knows everything?

For centuries, leadership was built on two key advantages:

1. An asymmetry of information
2. The ability to craft and express a visionary narrative—a compelling story that inspires people to follow

Those who led in business, politics, or warfare did so, in part, because they had access to knowledge that others didn't. Better intelligence (sharper insights and exclusive information) created opportunities for power.

Leadership relied on knowing more than anyone else and telling a compelling story about it.

Differentiating as a leader, in particular, involved leveraging that asymmetric access to information: taking what few knew, shaping it into an approachable, persuasive argument, and using it to educate, engage, and rally people toward some shared goal.

However, in modern times, the asymmetric knowledge advantage is fading fast as AI levels the playing field.

When artificial intelligence can instantly gather, analyze, and synthesize more data than any human mind could ever process, knowledge is no longer exclusive nor difficult to obtain.

That means access to information and insights is no longer a differentiator. The edge that once separated leaders from followers—the ability to see what others miss—fades.

When anyone can access the same insights, when every decision can be optimized and stress-tested by algorithms, and when the execution can be handled by autonomous systems, the question becomes, "What's left?"

Universal access to AI-driven knowledge seems to suggest two competing outcomes:

- **Greater consensus**. If everyone sees the same reliable information, people might converge on shared truths, allowing reason and evidence to guide decisions. This outcome requires a critical-minded society that can separate credible data from unreliable sources.

- **Post-truth polarization**. Conversely, if the volume of "facts" becomes overwhelming, leaders (and their followers) can cherry-pick data that support preconceived beliefs. This outcome fosters a post-truth environment in which factual consensus becomes nearly impossible. When each faction claims to espouse the "real facts," truth becomes contested—and the loudest or most persuasive voice may win.

It's pretty clear that early results point toward the latter outcome in our culture. Today, the most influential person in the room isn't necessarily the one with the best information—just the one with the biggest megaphone, the hottest take, or the most unhinged presentation.

The Value is in the Boundaries

Whatever we think about AI and its evolution, the trend is becoming clear: it will be the biggest disruption to leadership, knowledge, and differentiation that we've seen in centuries.

But the early results also point to most people using AI and automation technology to focus on speed and getting faster access to knowledge; still trying for that asymmetry of information. But that, literally, can't last. So, perhaps the way to focus on differentiation is to utilize modern technology in a different way. Perhaps we can wrestle with the idea that *differentiation lives at the boundary, between the layers, where people still do the reasoning and exploring but use AI to help them see things they hadn't noticed before.*

Are you starting to see how that's friction?

If you think of AI as an intern focused on derivative output, you expect it to provide fast, helpful (but shallow and predictable) work. If you treat AI as a full-on replacement for human agency, it still falls short. It lacks taste, judgment, and wisdom. At the other extreme, that thinking leads to the expectation of the mythical "single-person company"—the so-called "vibe leader"—wearing an augmented reality headset and orchestrating a swarm of agentic bots. Congratulations, you've just created a single point of failure that lives and dies with your every decision. For everything.

But what if you don't think of generative AI as something to help you go faster or do more? What if AI becomes the thing that allows you to *slow down*? To pause. To reflect. To shape better questions. To think more deeply about what you're making—and why.

Maybe this is the innovation that breaks the 25-year quest for more and more speed.

Maybe the true opportunity is to *decelerate* with intention.

The question for the differentiated leader then isn't, "What can AI help me execute?" And it's not, "What can AI do that I can't?"

It's: *"What might I explore now that I couldn't see before?"*

That's the boundary. That's where the strategy shifts from velocity to depth.

This is a core idea from epistemology, the philosophy of knowledge. The philosophy is, basically, the thinking of why we know what we know. It's not only about accuracy but also about justification.

The question "Why do we believe this?" matters most at the boundary of understanding, where confidence is low and uncertainty is high.

Say you're watching a medical documentary claiming a diet improves brain health. It sounds convincing with all the charts, expert quotes, and a cited study or two. Though you're not a neurologist, you've read enough to ask questions like "Is this correlation or causation?" or "Was this a clinical trial or an observational study?"

You might even agree with the charts and experts. But that moment of questioning is epistemology in action. You're not unquestioningly accepting what sounds smart. You're interrogating what seems plausible.

But epistemology doesn't stop at the question. It pushes us to evaluate the reasoning, seek context, and understand what evidence would justify belief.

That's the part the current framing of AI skips over.

When AI surfaces a pattern or suggests a strategy, your job isn't to take it at face value. It's to ask, "Could this be right?"

That's not outsourcing judgment. That's practicing it. In this model, AI doesn't think for you. It helps *you* think more completely.

The Paradox of AI-Driven Leadership

AI won't just change how decisions are made—it will alter what leadership requires. Remember, leadership was never *just* about access to information. It also depended on persuasion, storytelling, and charisma—qualities that aligned people toward a shared vision.

To draw it back to the monks and my time at Showtime Networks: It's not just that the monks or I had to access to the information—it was that we were able to create meaningful experiences with it. The monks created universities, I created PowerPoints. Not quite the same thing, but you get the point.

But, wait, what if we subscribe to the idea that "Today's AI is the dumbest you'll ever use?" Okay, so what happens as AI evolves and reduces the need for people to not just express ideas but to also execute tasks based on them?

We're already seeing workforce reductions in information-based roles, with AI increasingly positioned as the replacement. If future AI agents churn out thought leadership content *and* carry out executive decisions without question or pushback from humans, does differentiated leadership shift from inspiring and mobilizing people to merely making wise decisions?

Whether you're publishing AI-generated thought leadership or making high-stakes business decisions, a lack of human challenge increases the risk. Without pushback, scrutiny, or debate, even the best-intentioned decisions go untested—opening the door to blind spots and systemic failures.

This creates an intriguing leadership paradox:

- **The rise of low-ego, highly analytical leaders.** As AI takes over execution, leadership may become less about charisma, emotion, and persuasion and more about wisdom, ethics, and discernment (precision decision-making). These leaders will succeed not because they can captivate a room or rally a team but because they consistently make sound, well-reasoned choices.

- **A greater need for deeply human, charismatic leaders.** As AI renders decisions increasingly cold and clinical, people may crave the opposite—leaders who make them feel something. In a world drowning in data, trust in a leader's judgment and integrity may become more important than their knowledge or abilities. People might ask, *"Do I believe you are using this information in my best interest?"* rather than *"What information do you have that I don't?"*

Think about it: On one end, you get hyper-logical, Spock-like leaders who are efficient and precise but detached from human emotion. On the other, you get magnetic, larger-than-life personalities who captivate and inspire but prioritize charisma over substance.

Maybe the real challenge is finding leadership that blends the best of both without falling into either trap.

The Future of Differentiated Leadership: What Can We Do?

AI has further democratized information. Therefore, the future of leadership can't simply be about unique insights. It has to involve unique perspectives that foster trust and build deeper relationships.

All these questions suggest that, to become differentiated, leaders should consider shifting their focus in three crucial ways:

1. **Stop delivering mere facts and start shaping emotional meaning.** AI can generate endless information, but leadership won't be about producing more information—it will be about guiding interpretation. Said another way, the true value of thought leadership will not lie in simply expressing a big idea that everyone consumes. It will lie in helping *different groups* contextualize and synthesize the same insights in ways that create broader, shared understanding and deeper meaning across the different groups.

    Put even more simply: the goal in solving puzzles will not be to hand individual groups of people a brand-new puzzle only they can solve. It's to fit all the pieces together so everyone sees one big, shared picture—so that we can all say, "Aha, we get it!" It's not just about presenting data; it's about framing it in a way that fosters trust, alignment, and action across groups.

2. **Remember that trust in the storyteller is the foundation of**

belief in the story. John Maxwell once wrote that People buy into the leader before they buy into the vision ... leaders cannot take their people to places they haven't yet traveled to themselves!"[12] In other words, the story creates value and builds trust, but if an audience doesn't believe in the storyteller, the message loses its impact.

3. **Create more interactive and community-driven experiences.** The new thought leadership objective isn't just broadcasting for attention or consumption; it's about engagement, interactivity, and co-creation. Loyalty over transactions. Depth over virality. Instead of simply broadcasting insights, thought leaders must foster conversations, cultivate communities, and create collaborative spaces where ideas don't just spread but also evolve.

Elevating trusted voices and helping them grow into the leaders of tomorrow is one of our most crucial tasks. Thought leadership is no longer just about dispensing unique information—it's about the credibility, integrity, and authenticity of the people behind it.

If these three ideas turn out to be true, the future of differentiated leadership won't rest on an asymmetry of information—because information is now universally accessible. Nor will it rely solely on charisma, broad influence, or some iconoclastic provocation.

Instead, leadership will hinge on the ability to create an *asymmetry of relationships* in which leaders not only broadcast insights but also imbue them with deeper meaning, context, and trust and find ways to co-create within varied and specific communities. It's not about having exclusive knowledge and making it widely available; it's about shaping understanding in a way that resonates, builds credibility, and fosters genuine connection in very specific contexts.

And the way to get there? Valuable Friction.

Friction as a Signal of Knowing

Leadership in the age of AI won't be defined by what you know or even what you can do. Those advantages are disappearing. What remains, and what will endure, is your ability to hold space for trust, for meaning, and for motion through complexity.

That requires friction.

Friction is what allows asymmetry of relationships to exist with integrity. It's what gives someone the *right* to lead—not because they know more, but because they've done the work to build something deeper with the people around them.

In a world where people can access any information, differentiated leadership won't be about having the answer. A differentiated leader will be the one who takes the time to carry the weight of the answer. To feel its implications. To translate it. To stand by it when it matters most.

That's what Valuable Friction does. It slows down the moment enough to let the relationship hold more weight than the insight. It reminds us that leading isn't a performance—it's a practice.

Leadership in this new era won't involve commanding authority. It will require leaders to earn it one community at a time. The ones who thrive won't be those who control but those who connect.

Leadership isn't about seeing the path anymore. It's about making the journey matter.

CHAPTER 4

Deliberately Different

The Four Frictions that Keep your Work from Melting into Meh

> *"I watch the ripples change their size*
> *But never leave the stream of warm impermanence and*
> *So the days float through my eyes*
> *But still the days seem the same..."*
>
> —David Bowie, "Changes"

There's a cliché (and yeah, some stereotypes exist for a reason) that strategy consultants and agencies often recommend plans that teams can't actually implement.

The proposed changes might be too complex, too expensive, too disruptive, or too long-term to feel real. You've heard the jokes: the one about measuring a strategy by the sound it makes when you drop it on the table. Or how business leaders keep their bookshelves lined with decks that were never executed.

So why does that cliché persist? Why do so many strategies never make it off the shelf?

Well, the teams being consulted often complain that the strategist—whether external or internal—didn't understand the realities of their situation. Meanwhile, the consultant walks away muttering that the client "just didn't get it" or "wasn't ready for an optimal strategy."

And there's the word: *optimal*.

In reality, both sides are a little bit right—and a little bit wrong. The consultant probably *didn't* fully grasp the history, constraints, or energy of the team. And the team probably wasn't (and may never be) in a place to implement the perfect strategy as written.

But no consultant in their right mind sets out to build a *suboptimal* strategy. Or…do they?

And no client ever jumps on Zoom to say, "You know what? Skip the ideal plan—we'd like the good-enough-for-us version." Or…should they?

That's the stalemate. It's similar to that weird cultural habit where we conflate struggle with significance, which I explore in "The Friction Balance Curve". Only, in this case, it's not just about individual narratives. It's about two sides posturing around what's "optimal" when neither wants to admit that *good enough would be a massive improvement and optimal might actually be wrong.*

So, we avoid the truth. It's easier. It's faster. We rationalize the mismatch. And we say things like, "You just don't get me," instead of saying, "Let's figure out what's right for us."

This is the trap. We assume the "optimal" thing is something we have to *live up to*, instead of asking whether it's something we can *live with*. We confuse the vision with the version we can actually carry out.

But what if, in this case, we introduced just the right kind of friction and set ourselves apart—not by prescribing perfection but by shaping something together?

As any good consultant would also do, let me make this about me for a second and give you an example.

A while back, I wrapped a long consulting engagement and asked my client for a testimonial. What they said caught me off guard.

"You're just…a different kind of consultant."

At first, I wasn't sure how to take it. Was that praise? Or a polite critique? It's like when someone hears your take, squints a little, tilts their head, and says, "Huh…that's interesting." You're left wondering if that means "fascinating" or "please stop talking".

He assured me that he meant it as a compliment. But it was only after I sat with it—and looked back at the work I'd done—that I think I understood what he meant.

I'd been hired to help restructure their marketing operation. On paper, it was a classic project: realign the workflow, clarify roles, improve governance, streamline editorial. But pretty quickly, nothing about it felt straightforward.

The creative team felt boxed in. Leadership wanted speed. Ops was stuck between systems. Technology felt unheard. And underneath it all was the real, unspoken tension: *Could they actually change any of this?*

At times, it felt slow. Messy. Tense. But then something started to emerge.

The creative tension helped us clarify what they were really trying to say. The strategic pauses let us ask better questions. The operational mess forced us to slow down and build something sustainable. The "best practice" frameworks I introduced were just starting points for a discussion, not a "standard" to live up to. The relational friction made space for truth—and trust.

By the end, it wasn't about the plan, or the workflow, or the slides, or even the frameworks I handed over. The real value was in the experience they had *with themselves*. They didn't install a system I had architected. They *lived into* a system they had helped create.

And what they walked away with wasn't a strategy. It was confidence. Conviction. Ownership.

This didn't happen *in spite* of the friction. It was *because of it.* And that made the work different.

I tell you that story not because I think the work was better—or more important—than what another consultant might have done. Someone else could have delivered a strong result a different way. But what I do know is this: the experience felt different. And that difference helped me stand out to this one client—and to others he referred me to.

I also tell you that story because, well, I'm a consultant at heart, which means I have a framework. So, just know that what follows isn't meant to be prescriptive. It's not a badge or a checklist or a claim of mastery. It's just my way of framing things. A language. A system you can live into, revise, and make your own.

A Practice of Friction

Over the last few years of thinking about this, I started to notice that friction didn't always show up the same way. Sometimes it came through a creative constraint. Sometimes it showed up as a strategic delay. Other times it was built into a team's rhythm—or lived inside a conversation that felt just uncomfortable enough to be honest. That's when I began to see it not only as a theme, but as a connected framework.

Not a formula. A lens. A way of noticing where friction is doing useful work—and how we might apply it with more care and intention. But these four forms of friction aren't just categories of work. They're interconnected human capacities.

4 Forms of Valuable Friction

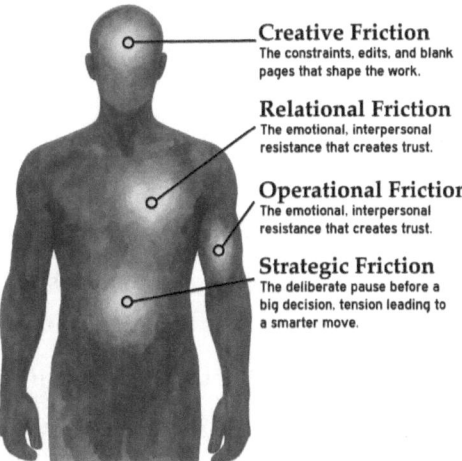

Creative Friction
The constraints, edits, and blank pages that shape the work.

Relational Friction
The emotional, interpersonal resistance that creates trust.

Operational Friction
The emotional, interpersonal resistance that creates trust.

Strategic Friction
The deliberate pause before a big decision, tension leading to a smarter move.

- **Creative Friction** is the mind—where constraints, edits, and blank pages refine our ideas and sharpen originality.
- **Operational Friction** is the muscle—the structure, repetition, and rituals that make progress durable.
- **Relational Friction** is the heart—the emotional tension that, when navigated well, deepens trust and connection.
- **Strategic Friction** is the soul—the inner compass that slows us down long enough to choose wisely and move with clarity.

Each has its role. But they don't work alone.

- Mind without heart can be clever but cold.
- Muscle without direction burns out fast.
- Heart without grounding can drown in emotion.
- Soul without motion stays stuck in potential.

Together, they form a more complete way of being—not just at work, but in life. Valuable Friction is how we bring our whole selves into the picture. It's how we deliberately shape more meaning in a world obsessed with momentum.

My idea is that this isn't just a productivity framework or a personal branding tool. It's a way to reconsider how we live, how we lead, and how we create. It offers a structure to counterbalance a culture that too often values seamlessness over substance and speed over meaning.

When we treat these not just as tactics but as an integrated way of being, they reinforce each other. Mind, heart, soul, and muscle—working together to shape not just better outcomes, but deeper meaning.

Across all of them, what holds true is this: A little purposeful resistance—a pause, a question, a challenge—is often what sparks something worth remembering.

Friction, when designed with care, isn't an obstacle. It's a lever.

Grounded in Pace Layering

To ground this idea even further, I would note that I was inspired by one of the most useful long-term thinking frameworks of the last half-century: Stewart Brand's Pace Layering Model.

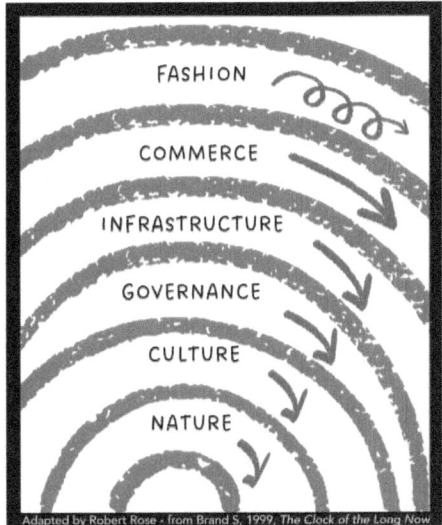

Brand proposed that society is comprised of layers that move at different speeds and serve different purposes. Their interaction is what keeps systems stable and adaptable over time.

"Fast learns, slow remembers," Brand wrote. "Fast proposes, slow disposes."

The Pace Layering Model has always stuck with me—probably because it doesn't try to explain how change happens in one sweeping arc. Instead, it shows how change lives in layers. Different tempos. Different kinds of motion.

Some layers move fast, like fashion or commerce. As Brand said, "It is culture cut free to experiment as creatively and irresponsibly as the society can bear."[13]

Honestly, that quote has become one of the inspirations behind the timing of this book—because I think that's exactly where we are as a culture. We've hit the unbearable limit. The pace of creativity, and the degree of irresponsibility we're tolerating around it, has reached a saturation point.

But other layers move slowly—like infrastructure, governance, or the deeper strata of culture. And the brilliance of Brand's model is how it maps the tension between the fast and the slow. Between what must adapt quickly and what must hold firm. If everything moved at the speed of fashion, we'd live in chaos. If everything moved at the speed of infrastructure, we'd be paralyzed.

Pace Layering isn't just a philosophical idea—it's a design for durability. It helps us see how different parts of our world absorb shocks, maintain coherence, and build resilience. It helps us align short-term experimentation with long-term stability. It reminds us how to honor what's slow without denying what needs to move.

And that, I think, is where Valuable Friction fits in.

Valuable Friction happens at the boundaries—at the interfaces between these layers. It lives in the tension between what's accelerating and what's holding steady. And learning how to work with that tension—intentionally, and with care—is where the real work (and the real opportunity) lives.

Each form of Valuable Friction can be understood as emerging from a similar kind of interface:

Form of Friction	Related Pace Layer(s)	Interaction Insight
Creative Friction	Fashion/Art vs. Culture	Creativity thrives in the push between novelty and meaning.
Strategic Friction	Commerce vs. Governance	Smart decisions arise when your speed is tempered by broader consequences.
Operational Friction	Infrastructure	Quality work relies on processes that resist haste.
Relational Friction	Governance vs. Culture	Trust emerges slowly, through tension and resolution.

Friction, in this sense, is the interface mechanism that keeps layers in dialogue. It's the resistance that allows different tempos to synchronize just enough to move forward without breaking.

And just as Brand's framework helps us understand how civilization holds itself together, the Four Forms of Valuable Friction help us design better systems of attention, trust, and value in our own lives and work.

Because maybe, just maybe…"optimal" isn't really the point.

Not the biggest idea. Not the fastest plan. Not the most polished deck. Just the thing that fits—because it was built with care. Because it was shaped through a little resistance. Because it holds up, not in theory but in use.

That's the kind of difference Valuable Friction creates. It's not "optimal" friction—it's just valuable. It doesn't try to be perfect for everyone. It tries to be *right*—for the people it's meant to serve, for the moment it's meant to meet.

Maybe, just maybe, that's what can set us apart—not just in what we build, but in how we build it. The pauses we make. The pressure we hold. The details we choose not to smooth away.

CHAPTER 5

Creative Friction

Constraints, Tension, and the Alchemy of Turning Limits into Lightning

> *"But me, I'm still on the road*
> *Headin' for another joint*
> *We always did feel the same*
> *We just saw it from a different point of view"*
>
> —Bob Dylan, "Tangled Up in Blue"

It's a well-worn phrase: *creativity loves constraints*. And while it's often tossed around as a kind of motivational shorthand, it speaks to something deeper—and truer—than it's usually given credit for.

Because in the real, messy process of making something—whether it's a story, a product, a strategy, or a moment that resonates—ease is not usually the goal. In fact, the creative act lives in the tension between possibility and limitation.

This is the work of the mind. Not just the part that dreams, but the part that wrestles. That sorts. That sharpens. Creative Friction is the mental resistance that transforms raw ideas into real ones. It's where constraint becomes clarity—and where edits, critiques, and even blank pages do their quiet work of shaping something better.

To be clear, the act of creativity isn't just about making a thing, a "work." It can be about ideas, strategies, the life you lead. So, if you think this motion isn't for you because you're not a "creative," then I refer you to the words of the wonderfully creative music producer Rick Rubin, who said in his book *The Creative Act*:

"What you make doesn't have to be witnessed, recorded, sold, or encased in glass for it to be a work of art. Through the ordinary state of being, we're already creators in the most profound way, creating our experience of reality and composing the world we perceive."[14]

We don't do our best thinking when everything is available to us instantly, without boundary or resistance. We do our best thinking when we're pressed to make choices. When we have to navigate uncertainty. When we can't do everything—so we must do *something* that matters.

Creative Friction shows up in many forms: the constraints we work within, the blank page that resists us, the editor who pushes back, the deadline that forces a decision, the tension of collaboration, the self-imposed rule that becomes the style.

Why Constraints Spark—Not Stifle—Creativity

The idea that limitation can lead to liberation isn't just a poetic contradiction—it's a creative truth that shows up across disciplines, from art to architecture to software design to that birthday party you're planning for your significant other.

At first, constraints seem like a creative enemy. They reduce options. They close doors. They say no. But very often, that's exactly what makes something original possible. Because too much freedom is its own kind of trap. When everything is possible, nothing feels necessary.

Psychologist Barry Schwartz described this dynamic in his 2004 book *The Paradox of Choice*. With too many options, we become overwhelmed, indecisive, even paralyzed. The same holds true in the creative process. Unlimited inputs rarely lead to focused, meaningful output. What sparks clarity is the moment we're forced to choose—or are forced by design to operate within a defined edge.[15]

This is why the blank page is so often feared. It offers total freedom—and zero direction. There's nothing to push against, nothing to shape the impulse. But once a single parameter is introduced—word count, tone, audience, format—ideas begin to organize themselves. Possibility becomes intent.

There's even a psychological term for this. *Productive constraint*—a close cousin to what we're calling creative friction—has been shown to increase divergent thinking. Psychologist Patricia Stokes, in her book *Creativity from Constraints*, observed that when creators are given some boundaries (for example: use only certain materials or work within a specific time frame), they often produce more inventive solutions than when they're given no guidelines at all.[16]

This is the heart of creative friction: a challenge, a boundary, a rule, or a resistance that forces focus. It makes the creator ask: *What matters here? What can I do with what I have? How do I turn less into more?*

It's not romanticizing struggle for struggle's sake. It's recognizing that the best work often needs a frame—because creativity isn't just expression. It's selection. It's subtraction. It's making meaning under pressure.

The Difference Between Helpful Tension and Paralyzing Pressure

Of course, not all friction is helpful. And not all tension is productive.

There's a line—sometimes thin, often personal—between the kind of challenge that sharpens a creative edge and the kind that dulls it completely.

Between the pressure that helps you focus and the pressure that makes you freeze.

So let's just call it out.

- **Helpful tension creates movement.** It focuses attention. It helps you commit. It says, *this is the edge where something new might emerge.* Think of the constraint that makes a problem solvable. The deadline that brings clarity. The feedback that unlocks the next revision. These kinds of friction are creative allies—not because they make things easier, but because they make them real.
- **Paralyzing pressure, on the other hand, creates collapse.** It overwhelms the system. It introduces fear. It removes the conditions needed for creativity—like safety, space, and play. Too much of it and we default to the obvious, or avoid the work altogether. We lose the signal under the weight of noise.

In other words: *it's not the presence of friction that matters—it's the kind of friction.* The creative process needs boundaries and tension, but it also needs support. It needs room to breathe. And that room to breathe is itself a kind of friction—especially if the pressure is to create as fast as possible.

This is where process design matters. This is where culture matters. Because a team—or an individual—doesn't need endless flexibility. But it does need permission to *stay in the work long enough* to find something original. That might mean a clear brief, a tight timeline, and a shared agreement that "rough is okay to start." It might mean rituals for editing, checkpoints for feedback, or a whiteboard rule that says every idea gets ten minutes before being dismissed.

Helpful friction is friction that's held. It's not dropped on people like weight. It's built into the system as a way of saying: *this matters enough to make space for it to be hard.*

You can see this playing out in real time with generative AI. Today, anyone can create a perfectly polished image or video "in the style of" any famous artist—in minutes. And yes, that might get the job done in a fast way. But what's gained in speed is lost in distinction. It's not really yours. It's not pushing you to find something new—it's referencing what's already been done.

While that kind of tool might be a brilliant sketching partner (actually helping you to create constraints), the real creative work still happens in the friction that follows: the decisions you make after the first draft. The discomfort of not quite knowing what you're solving for. The tension of finding your voice instead of mimicking someone else's. That's where you differentiate—not just in the thing that you make, but in the differentiation of you as the creator.

How Friction Helps Original Work Emerge (and Prevents Derivative Output)

One of the quiet dangers of a frictionless creative process is how easily it leads us to make things that feel…familiar. Polished. Efficient. And forgettable.

We've all felt it. When the work flows too fast, it often flows right past the part where something could have taken shape. That moment when you could have paused. Changed direction. Asked a better question. But the process didn't ask anything of you. It was too smooth to leave a mark.

This is one of the defining tensions of modern creative work in a world of generative AI and automation. On one hand, we have unprecedented tools for speed and scale. On the other, we're drowning in derivative content—articles that sound the same, designs that blur together, brand voices that all start to feel like they went to the same corporate retreat.

For example: When you're shaping thought leadership, crafting a story, developing a brand message, or writing a proposal—you're probably not asking, "What's my data strategy?"

Of course not. But AI is.

Generative AI has blurred the lines between content and data. To AI providers, your articles, novels, podcasts, and/or videos (whatever you've poured your heart into) are not creative work. They're training data: indexed, deconstructed, and reassembled, not for meaning, but for pattern.

This perspective isn't new. It's rooted in the logic of search engine indexes, where frequency and correlation determine relevance. In that world, content was already reduced to data—and nobody pretended search engines understood what they were indexing.

But now, AI systems are being anthropomorphized, described as having intuition. Insight. Understanding.

Let's be clear: AI doesn't understand meaning, it understands data. It expresses what we see as meaning as the most probable data based on the data it has been trained on.

It generates the most probable next word, or pixel, or note, based on a statistical relationship to all the data it's ingested. We often complain that AI creates "average" content—meaning not very good quality. But it's not producing "average" work. It's producing what's *most likely* to be next. That's very different. And it's why meaning, which depends on context and intent, still belongs to humans.

This is the creative friction.

Because when you let AI generate something "in the style of …" without interrogating what that means—what it erases, what it repeats—you may win the speed battle. But you lose the opportunity to say something that's actually yours.

This isn't just theoretical.

In one study, consumers responded less positively to emotionally resonant content they believed was created by AI than to identical content that was human-created. Another study found that people could only identify AI-generated text 53% of the time—barely better than a coin flip. The takeaway? Even if your audience can't detect it, your brand—or your voice—may suffer when what you're creating feels unearned or unexamined.

Because AI is producing the most probable content, the quality may be amazing, or completely wrong, or just awful. So, the danger of defaulting to AI and speed in the creative process is not that it produces bad, or average, content. It's that it may erode *your* ability to know the difference. If you can't tell whether what it produced is brilliant, derivative, or just wrong, you've ceded the very thing that sets you apart: discernment.

Let me be clear about my own position. This doesn't mean AI has no place in the creative process. I use it all the time—for thumbnails, mock-ups, meme templates, early-stage sketching. For anything meant to be disposable or iterative, it's a fantastic partner.

But here's the sticky bit: the moment we start talking "ethics," the debate usually collapses into a yes-or-no quiz—did you use AI or not? That framing is like asking, "*How many grains of sand until you have a pile?*" One swipe of the hand and the line blurs. A single AI-generated sentence inside a 2,000-word article: is that still "human" work? What about a reference image that trained the mood board? The binary breaks down fast.

So instead of policing the exact grain count, let's shift the questions we can ask ourselves:

1. **Intent:** Am I using the tool to clarify my thinking—or to dodge the thinking entirely?
2. **Transparency:** Would the audience feel misled if they knew the recipe?
3. **Accountability:** Am I still on the hook for the outcome, or am I hiding behind the algorithm when things go sideways?

Follow those three checkpoints and the ethical line sorts itself out. In other words: use the sand, build the castle—just don't pretend the tide didn't help.

I understand the balance of friction for what I'm trying to do in any given creative process. In all cases when I use AI, its output is the *least* interesting thing. If it's just a thumbnail image for a podcast episode, I might use what it puts out. But if I'm trying to differentiate (oh, let's say in helping me conceptualize the Friction Curve Framework), then I put a question mark at the end of whatever AI output I get for my prompt. How does it make ME wrestle harder with the idea?

That wrestling takes time. It takes friction. It takes a process that asks more than, "What's fastest?" and instead asks, "What's true?" or "What's mine to say?"

That's where creative friction lives. It doesn't just help us avoid the obvious. It helps us escape it entirely.

Practical Ways to Build Creative Friction into Your Process

Creative Friction doesn't require heroic suffering. You don't need to move to a cabin, write longhand by candlelight, or invent elaborate constraints just to feel like the work is real.

But let's get practical for a moment.

As I mentioned earlier, I don't want you to see the word "creative" and immediately think, "Oh, that's not for me—I'm not a writer or a designer." Creative Friction isn't necessarily about making a thing. It's about making *anything* with intention. If you're shaping something, solving something, or simply rethinking how to express an idea, this applies to you.

The idea of "making time" to be creative isn't new. For the last twenty-five years, humans have faced a steady push to express ideas faster. But with the rise of generative AI, we've officially reached peak speed.

And with that speed comes pressure. Students, managers, artists—everyone is being nudged to move faster, publish more often, speak sooner. To opt for the ease that technology enables.

It's tempting to comfort ourselves with the idea that "faster than humans" isn't the same as replacing humans. And maybe that's true. But let's be honest: as the technology gets smarter and smarter, that reassurance sometimes feels like that wood panel Kate Winslet and Leonardo DiCaprio were clinging to in the water in *Titanic*. It looks big enough to save everyone—but somehow, it doesn't.

So, what's the move?

It's not about retreating to analog purity or outsourcing everything to automation. It's about balance. Discernment. Creative judgment.

One of the most useful ways I've found to hold that balance is with a simple lens: the difference between something constructed and something created.

G.K. Chesterton said it best in his reflection on *The Pickwick Papers*:

"The whole difference between construction and creation is exactly this: that a thing constructed can only be loved after it is constructed; but a thing created is loved before it exists."[17]

Created expression is the poem that forms in your mind before the pen ever touches paper. It's the painting you see in your head before the brush hits the canvas. It's the article that takes shape in an outline, deepens through research, and lands in a sentence that finally says what you mean.

Constructed expression, by contrast, gains value only *after* it's been built. A street sign. A meme. A product description. A podcast thumbnail. A project status email. No one, including the creator, anticipates them with excitement—but they're useful and necessary once they exist.

AI excels at constructed content. But it doesn't create in the way humans do. It doesn't feel the spark of an idea before it takes form. It doesn't nurture, shape, or love what it's making. That's our job. That's the work.

And it matters, because the real value of created content isn't just in how it performs. It's in what it gives back to the creator. When people create, they don't just produce something—*they* change in the process. They live with an idea. Wrestle with it. Shape it. They become part of the work and the work becomes part of them.

This matters not just philosophically, but practically. Your inner CEO might say, "I don't care how the creative team feels about the process as long as the output works." But here's what you (and your inner CEO) should care about: the bottom line.

Wiser, more engaged creators aren't just happier. They're more profitable. Because while AI follows instructions perfectly, humans get better and better at writing the next, unexpected set of instructions. They anticipate problems. They connect the dots others don't. They generate the ideas and decide what should express them: a picture, words, video, audio, or even a physical experience.

That's why creative friction matters. When someone is engaged—when they're wrestling with ideas—they're not just completing tasks. They're inventing better ways to do them.

That's not just valuable. It's irreplaceable.

Here's the thing I speak to businesses about all the time: If you believe AI will allow us to do more with fewer people, then you also have to believe that it can allow us to do more meaningful work with the same, or more, people. Why are we so willing to choose the former and unwilling to fight for the latter?

The best investment in generative AI isn't what it replaces. It's what it unlocks.

When you use it to augment rather than replace human creativity, you don't just create better content—you create a better creator.

With that lens in mind, here are a few ways to bring more creative friction into your process—not as punishment, but as practice.

Tactics for Constructing or Creating with Intention

- **Impose a Creative Constraint**

  Choose one meaningful limit: a word count, a palette, a timebox, a format, a tone.

  The goal isn't to narrow the idea—it's to give it form. Think of *Green Eggs and Ham*, written with just 50 words. Or Jack White limiting himself to analog gear and three colors. Simpler isn't always smaller. It's sharper.

- **Build In a Pause**

  Add a deliberate moment of reflection before you call something finished. Sleep on the draft. Sit with the design. Ask someone—even your AI tool—to poke holes in it. Create a 24-hour "cooling off" step before you ship your expressed idea—not to slow momentum, but to make space for a better question.

- **Start Messy**

  Give yourself permission to begin with something unclear, undercooked, or weird. High friction often shows up as resistance to imperfection. But iteration is your friend. The mess is the map.

- **Invite a Contrarian**

  Creative tension is often missing because everyone's being too polite. Bring in someone who'll challenge the idea—not to kill it, but to strengthen it. Their resistance is a form of care. The friction they bring might be the edge that makes the work unforgettable.

- **Don't Automate the Meaningful Part**

    Use tools to speed up the repetitive stuff. But keep the defining moments human—the judgment, the shaping, the nuance. Those are the parts worth wrestling with.

Creative Friction doesn't guarantee brilliance, but it creates the conditions where brilliance becomes possible. And that's because it doesn't just help us make better things.

It helps us become part of what we've made.

It makes the work matter. To the audience, sure. But more importantly, to us.

CHAPTER 6

Strategic Friction

Pauses, Pushback, and the Decision-Making Friction that Differentiates

"You can't start a fire without a spark
This gun's for hire
Even if we're just dancin' in the dark"

—Bruce Springsteen, *"Dancing in the Dark"*

In fast-paced environments—whether it's figuring out where to go with your career after college, launching a startup, running a small nonprofit, or navigating a global enterprise—modern strategy is often treated like a tempo issue. The assumption baked into our culture since the early 2000s—though not necessarily true—is that faster thinking is better thinking. Responsiveness is always a virtue. Momentum is its own kind of clarity.

But real clarity doesn't always come from speed. It comes from alignment. From sensing. From the pause that gives our decisions room to breathe.

Strategic Friction is the soul of the system—the gut-level resistance that asks us to sit with tension just long enough to find a better way forward.

It's not paralysis. It's discernment. The subtle, steady kind of knowing that doesn't shout, but guides.

In this chapter, we'll explore how slowing down—intentionally, not reactively—can turn hesitation into wisdom and strategy into something more than just a plan: Something that feels *true*.

There is a common mantra today that goes: move fast and break things.

Perhaps the more common misunderstanding is the belief that speed and agility are the same thing—especially when it comes to strategy. Ask someone who's fixated on moving fast and they'll often tell you they're being agile. But they're not. The two are different in ways that matter. Speed is the ability to move quickly in a straight line. Agility is the ability to change direction gracefully, responsively, under pressure. One increases when friction is removed. The other depends on it being there.

In a September 2024 episode of the *Acquired* podcast, Meta CEO Mark Zuckerberg drew a contrast between Meta's strategy and Apple's. He said:

"We're the opposite of Apple. They take a long time, they polish things, and then they put it out. Maybe that works for them."[18]

The implication? Apple moves slowly; we move fast.

But what's interesting is how visibly Zuckerberg struggles during this eight minute segment to articulate the difference between *speed* and *strategic adaptation*. When challenged on whether "speed" just means releasing suboptimal work, he backtracks: "Well, I don't want to overstate it …"

Eventually, he lands on what he actually means:

"Product strategy is about learning and iterating as fast as possible … If we can learn faster than everyone else, we'll win."[19]

And that's the real insight: not speed for speed's sake, but the ability to process and pivot faster than others. In other words: intentional agility.

But here's the twist—most of the coverage missed that distinction. The comments, headlines, and hot takes all echoed the same sentiment of what they learned from Zuck's interview:

"Speed is everything in business."

Spoiler alert: it isn't.

The Pitfalls of Reckless Velocity

"Move fast and break things" was a developer slogan. Then it became a business plan. Then a cultural blueprint. Speed was the virtue. Disruption was the aesthetic. Caution was the enemy.

And sure, in the early days of product development, moving quickly helped teams learn faster, iterate faster, and stay ahead of competitors. Breakage wasn't failure—it was progress.

But then the mindset started showing up *everywhere*:

- **In business strategy**, it meant scaling at all costs. Startups were told to grow now and figure out profitability later.
- **In marketing and branding strategy**, it meant publishing constantly. Don't wait for a great idea—ship the fast one.
- **In culture and our approach to using products**, it meant we stopped expecting anything to be stable. Everything is in beta.
- **In the education of our children**, we praised precocity, not persistence. Testing replaced exploration. Bullet points replaced depth.
- **In relationships**, we optimized for speed and convenience. Swipe-based dating. Bullet-pointed Slack threads. Conflict resolution in the form of quick reactions and status updates.

We moved fast. And now, a decade later, we're all left looking around and asking: Why is everything broken?

Because the assumption that speed *equals* agility has taken us to the limits of our capacity to adapt. Not just in tech, but in how we think, collaborate, and lead.

From Iteration to Intention

Strategic speed isn't inherently bad. In fact, it's critical in certain moments—especially when responding to customers. As Jay Baer points out in his book *The Time to Win*, "Two-thirds of customers care as much about speed as they do about price."

But speed without structure creates chaos. And, ironically, it often *slows us down*—because we're making fast decisions that we eventually have to revisit.

The better alternative? What Zuckerberg finally got to: agility. And what we're talking about here: strategic friction.

Strategic Friction is what makes agility intentional. It's what lets you pivot with purpose.

At the heart of this is a mindset shift—from valuing fast, iterative motion to prioritizing deliberate, meaningful progress.

It requires us to pause long enough to ask:

- Why am I chasing another rebrand when we haven't committed to the one we already have?
- Why do I feel pressure to launch this side project now, when I haven't even defined success?
- Why am I rewriting the deck for the fifth time instead of having a real conversation?
- Why do I need to post three times a day when one good post might build trust?
- Why am I trying to "scale" something I haven't even tested with one actual person?

- Why do I feel the need to reply to this email tonight? Am I managing expectations or just managing my own anxiety?

Here's an example from business: In my marketing strategy work, I often recommend shifting from container-first thinking (e.g., "We need a white paper!") to story-first thinking. Get clear on what you're trying to say—*then* decide all the formats you might create. A white paper. A podcast. A short video. All of the above.

The pushback?

"That sounds like it's going to slow down the content calendar."
"Yes. But it'll speed up everything else that actually matters."

The Difference Between a Productive Pause and Decision Paralysis

In a world obsessed with speed, it's tempting to equate velocity with progress. However, the most successful organizations understand that real progress comes from moving with purpose.

To be clear, though, slowing down doesn't always sound like a strategy.

In many organizations, especially larger ones, pausing is still interpreted as hesitation. As inefficiency. As indecision. In a culture built around moving fast and staying busy, it can feel uncomfortable—even risky—to be the one who says, "Let's not rush this."

But there's a meaningful difference between a productive pause and a strategic stall-out. One creates clarity. The other creates confusion. Knowing the difference is essential to using friction well.

A productive pause:

- Names what it's for (alignment, reflection, risk analysis)
- Sets a clear boundary (timeframe, session, or decision point)
- Moves through tension, not around it

A paralyzing stall:

- Avoids the real issue
- Delays decisions without redefining them
- Lets energy leak instead of consolidating it

Strategic Friction doesn't drag out decisions. It sharpens them.

It says:

"Are we still solving the right problem?"
"Have we really earned this answer yet?"

Sometimes, friction is just an extra slide that says, "What we're *not* doing." Sometimes it's a team moment titled, "What are we avoiding?"

It doesn't always slow the work. But it often slows us just enough to make it matter.

Let Friction Improve the Decision

Strategic Friction isn't about making things harder.

It's about making things more honest. It's what keeps us from racing ahead simply because we can. It gives us the space to pause and ask better questions—and the patience to sit with those questions long enough to feel when the answer is right. Because the best strategies don't just move fast. They move like they *mean* it.

And friction—the strategic kind—is what makes that possible.

It's the subtle, grounding force that connects the soles of our feet to the soul of the decision.

It's what gives us the ability to change direction with intention—not just reactively shift because the path got messy but sense that something deeper is calling for a different move.

Without friction, motion becomes momentum for its own sake. With friction, we gain the confidence to stop, pivot, adapt, and continue forward with more clarity than we had before.

In the end, it's not about going faster.

It's about knowing *why* you're moving. And trusting your footing—and your gut—enough to change course when it matters most.

CHAPTER 7

Operational Friction

Rhythms and Rituals that Make How You Work Impossible to Copy

"It's a long way to the top if you wanna rock 'n' roll"

—*AC/DC, "It's a Long Way to the Top"*

Not all friction lives in ideas or decisions. Some of the richest resistance shows up in the doing—in how we structure our days, run our teams, live with our families, and shape the repeatable systems that make the work, well, *work*.

This is Operational Friction: the kind that lives in muscle. In the habits, rituals, routines, reviews, and processes that aren't designed for speed but for strength. For sustainability. For sanity.

Too often, we treat operations as a back-office (or back-of-the-brain) function—mechanical, logistical, secondary to the "real" work of strategy or creativity. But in truth, operational systems are where most of our intentions either *take root* or *fall apart*.

This is the friction that builds endurance. The kind that shows up day after day, rep after rep, helping us stay grounded in what matters—and giving our best ideas something strong enough to stand on.

Picture this:

A new parent stands in the kitchen, sleep-deprived, trying to pack a lunch, refill the diaper bag, send one work email, and explain to a toddler why you can't wear snow boots in July.

A recent graduate scrolls through job listings, all demanding five years' experience for entry-level roles, wondering how to start a career when nothing looks like a beginning.

An entrepreneur, alone at the kitchen table, stares at a blank dashboard—trying to prioritize tasks, keep the vision alive, and figure out how to make rent without losing their soul.

A team leader hits send on yet another Monday morning email, hoping it sparks momentum—and not just more status meetings.

Different roles. Different worlds. Same feeling: This is harder than it looks, and no one gave me a blueprint.

Most of us aren't short on ambition or creativity. We're short on architecture—the invisible scaffolding that makes our efforts coherent, sustainable, and repeatable. This is especially true in the modern world where there are so many competing ideas for what actually works. So, we now instinctively search the internet for productivity hacks, new tools, maybe a new calendar layout, or some self-help book that will provide a template. But what we're really looking for is a *system* that helps us hold onto what matters and execute it with clarity.

That's where operational friction comes in. It's not a hack, or a tool, or a self-help template. It's simply a way of starting to utilize time in a slightly different way.

We've been trained to treat friction in the way we work as failure—something to eliminate. We see it as slowing us down, or bureaucracy, or bloat.

But some forms of friction are valuable. They're the slowdowns that make space for intention. The resistances that reveal what's misaligned. The guardrails that keep the core from falling apart when everything gets loud.

When I work with my clients in marketing and branding, I call this "story ops." But really, it's life ops. It's what makes the difference between improvising your way through chaos and building something that can grow.

Don't Just Build Templates—Build Architecture

It's tempting to confuse a routine with a system or a format with a structure. We find something that works—an email template, a family calendar, a guru's "to-do list"—and we think: *Great. I've got my system now.*

But templates are surface level. Architecture runs deeper.

A template tells you *how something should look.* An architecture defines *how it should work*—and, more importantly, *why.* It's the connective tissue underneath the visible work. And without it, even the best efforts eventually collapse under their own weight.

Take a student building a résumé. Today, objective statements are replaced by search-engine optimized, concise summaries highlighting relevant skills and experience. Work histories are keyword-packed bullet points showcasing accomplishments and quantifiable results.

Today's applicants may have two or even three core versions of their résumés, tailor them specifically for targeted applications, and maintain these résumés in multiple formats—from LinkedIn and job platform formats to plain text formats to beautiful PDF files and even multi-media websites.

Put simply: for today's young professionals, résumé management is a content strategy operation that would rival the content strategy at a small business. But if these young managers haven't thought through what core story they're telling—what kind of arc they're trying to create over time—then they're not building a career. They're just filling in blanks.

Or consider a founder juggling social posts, sales calls, and product tweaks. Maybe they've got tools. Maybe they've even hired help. But if there's no architecture behind the way they work—no sense of sequencing, prioritization, or built-in logic—every day becomes a scramble, not a strategy.

Even at home we fall into the trap. A family chore chart? Great. But does it reflect your actual values about responsibility, togetherness, rhythm, and rest? Or is it just the kanban board that you stole from work with your kids' names on the sprints—a colorful version of control?

Templates are helpful. They reduce the cognitive load. They can give form to chaos. But without architectural clarity—without a framework that explains what goes where, why it matters, and how it connects—you're just decorating a house with no foundation.

Architecture introduces operational friction in the best way: it slows down the impulse to jump straight to output. It forces us to step back, zoom out, and ask: *Is the structure of our operation sound*?

When your architecture is clear:

- Your decisions feel less arbitrary.
- Your team's (or family's) expectations sync up without constant reminders.
- Your energy goes toward execution, not reorientation.

That's the difference between a routine that "feels good when you remember to do it" and a way of working that *keeps working even when life gets loud.*

You don't need more templates. You need an operating structure that gives your work coherence and your life some rhythm.

Friction Isn't a Flaw—It's the Spark

If architecture gives your way of working strength, tension gives it life.

We're conditioned to smooth things out. To optimize for ease. To fix the bottlenecks, reduce the load time, cut the friction. But some friction is the point—it's what makes things interesting. It's not a bug in the system. It's a feature of a meaningful one.

Think about a great film, a powerful novel, even a memorable conversation—none work without tension. There has to be something at stake. Some uncertainty. Some resistance to overcome. Otherwise, there's nothing to engage with and hold our attention.

It's the same in the operations of everyday life.

- The **student** needs deadlines—not because stress is good, but because structure without stakes doesn't build momentum. A little pressure makes the effort feel real.
- The **parent** sets boundaries—not just to enforce rules, but to give children a sense of orientation and identity. Without limits, there's no shape to freedom.
- The **team** needs disagreements—not necessarily conflict, but structured tension. Without it, there's no rigor. No chance to sharpen ideas or challenge groupthink.
- The **founder** needs reality checks—places (or people) where vision hits resource constraints or trade-offs force hard prioritization. Without constraint, everything feels possible…and nothing actually ships. In operational terms, tension isn't just emotional. It can be built into the process.

So what do these deadlines, boundaries, disagreements, or reality checks look like in real life? Here are some examples:

- Decision checklists that force trade-offs: "If we say yes to this, what are we saying no to?"
- Story briefs that *require* a moment of struggle and debate with the team before outlining the resolution.
- Weekly rituals that surface unfinished work—not to assign blame, but to face discomfort directly.

Friction here plays a protective role. It slows down the slide into autopilot. It protects against the soft decay of convenience. In fact, systems that feel *too smooth* are often the ones that start to break the moment things get unpredictable. They provide a fragile calm, easily shattered.

I've seen this play out with clients more times than I can count. One marketing team I worked with had everything dialed in—on paper. Slick workflows, automated approvals, pre-populated briefs. Everything moved quickly. Too quickly, in fact.

There was no pause for context. No friction built into the system to ask: *Is this the right story? Is this even worth making?*

So, they cranked out content. A lot of it. But when the market shifted—and suddenly they needed to rethink tone, relevance, and channel strategy—they didn't have the muscle for it. The system that had once felt efficient turned brittle. It collapsed under even a modest level of change.

The result? A scramble. Content had to be pulled mid-campaign. Teams argued over messaging. Approvals that once took hours stretched into weeks. All because the system was built for speed, not resilience.

That's the danger of ultra-smooth operations. You mistake glide for glide-path. But when the terrain changes, there's no traction.

Operational Friction, done right, builds tension into the bones of the system so it stays strong under pressure. It asks you to sit with uncertainty, wrestle with trade-offs, and name what's really at stake.

To be clear, this is not about manufacturing drama—whether it's with your teammates, your employees, or your family. But you *do* need to make space for friction that fuels focus.

Because if everything is smooth, nothing sticks.

Create the Operations— the Work Behind the Work

Great ideas don't fail because they're bad—they fail because the system around them can't support their weight. I've seen this play out time and again in my 25 years of working with businesses of all sizes.

We love the spark. The aha moment. The clever insight scribbled on a whiteboard. But ideas on their own are fragile. They need structure to survive and momentum to spread. That's where operational friction comes in.

To reiterate: operations don't mean bureaucracy. I'm not talking about process for the sake of process. I'm talking about developing a rhythm and choreography that lets your team (or your life) absorb complexity and still move forward.

Think of it this way:

- The **team leader** who carves out space for cross-functional retros, quarterly story planning, or friction mapping exercises isn't slowing things down. They're building the infrastructure that lets *the right work* keep flowing.

- The **student** who only studies when they feel motivated is playing a dangerous game. The one who builds a recurring review habit—even if it's clunky—is building an operational layer that makes success more likely.

- The **parent** who creates weekly rituals (Sunday planning, Friday night resets) reduces decision fatigue and gives the whole family a shared cadence to move to.

- The **founder** who sets intentional constraints—like "no meetings before 10 a.m." or "one strategic priority per week"—isn't being rigid. They're designing the operating system that lets them protect focus and sanity.

Operational Friction shows up here as a speed bump with a purpose. It forces you to:

- Clarify ownership.
- Revisit assumptions.
- Get real about capacity.

It's not glamorous. You won't find it on a homepage or pitch deck. But it's the reason some people can keep showing up with clarity and consistency while others burn out or drift off course.

One client I worked with thought they had an alignment issue because messaging kept getting watered down during content reviews. It turned out the real problem was operational: no one knew who owned the story once it hit production, so it got nibbled to death by cross-functional feedback.

They didn't need a new content strategy, or brand, or guideline document. They needed an operational approach: who approves what, when tension gets surfaced, how stories get tracked across formats, and when someone has the authority to say, "Nope, this piece is done."

Operations aren't the enemy of creativity. They're what make it possible to be creative *again and again* without reinventing your entire identity every quarter.

When the system works, the story travels. When the choreography is clear, the dance feels free.

Measure the System—What it Made and How it Was Made

The most misunderstood part of examining how we operate is figuring out how to tell if we're doing it well. Is the startup founder doing well because they hit their revenue target—even if they're exhausted, scattered, and on the verge of burnout? How about the student looking to graduate? Are they doing well because they met every study block on their calendar—even if they retained nothing? Or, is the parent doing well because the morning routine ran like clockwork—even if no one spoke a kind word on the way out the door?

The strategic planning ideas from the *Strategic Friction* motion are instructive here. Too often, we inherit someone else's blueprint—some guru's framework, a productivity influencer's color-coded calendar, a self-help book's "perfect week." And we judge our success by whether we lived up to it. Did we execute every block? Did we follow the template?

But the better question isn't *"Did I live up to the system?"* It's *"Can I live with this system?"*

Can I do this again next week without resenting it? Does this rhythm serve me or just punish me for not being someone else?

Measuring operations means resisting the urge to fetishize discipline and instead get honest about sustainability, usefulness, and alignment. Not just "Did I do the thing?" but "Did doing the thing help me become who I want to be?" and "Can I keep doing it?"

Most of us measure success by looking at the end result. The metrics. The output. The win.

Did we launch? Did we sell? Did we grow?

And sure, outcomes matter. But in an environment where speed is the default setting, what matters even more is whether your system can do it again—and do it better next time.

That's where operational friction shifts the lens.

It asks not just *did it work* but *did it work the way we intended?*

Think about how a film studio evaluates success. Yes, box office numbers matter. But so does whether the production hit its milestones. Whether the director could work within the budget. Whether the creative team could deliver on time without imploding. Most importantly, they ask: *Can we make the next film without starting from scratch?*

That's the hidden power of a good system—not just a good story, but a repeatable structure that protects the creative process *and* the people doing the work.

Operational Friction encourages us to measure success *not just by the result, but by the repeatability and resilience of the system that produced it.*

So instead of only asking:

- Did it ship?
- Did it land?
- Did we hit the goal?

We also ask:

- Did the process build momentum or drain it?
- Did we reinforce our values or compromise them?
- Did this improve our ability to deliver the next one?

In client work, I've seen teams celebrate a high-performing piece of content only to realize no one knows how it happened. There's no audit trail. No reusable pieces. No system learning. Just a spike on a graph and a lot of guesswork next time.

Friction changes that. It slows the rush to *next* and says: *Let's reflect. Let's document. Let's codify what worked.*

And when we measure not just the outcome but the system that made it possible, something else happens too:

We start investing in the team. In the family. In the group. In ourselves.

Measurement becomes more than a scoreboard. It becomes a signal that we're building capacity. That the system is not just producing results but raising the value of the people playing the game.

They don't just build to win. They build to last.

The Difference Between Support and Drag

Let's be real: "operations" rarely make the highlight reel. "Oooo, fun, let's work on our process," said no one ever.

"Process." It sounds like red tape, slowdowns, maybe a few too many meetings about meetings. So when you talk about building in operational friction, it can sound like you're trying to make things harder on purpose.

But that's not the goal.

At its best, an operational system isn't a restriction. It's scaffolding. It gives shape to creativity, consistency to chaos, and traction to teams (even if it's just you) trying to do something that matters. *It doesn't slow the work—it makes the right speed sustainable.*

What's the difference between supportive operations and bureaucratic drag?

Supportive operations:

- Reinforce clarity: *Who's doing what, when, and why?*
- Create consistency: Not sameness—*reliability.*
- Scale culture and embed values into workflows (e.g., "We always debrief" or "We don't skip QA").
- Foster alignment: Fewer decisions need to be escalated.
- Encourage feedback: The system can evolve as the people in it do.

Bureaucratic drag:

- Obscures ownership: *Too many layers, unclear accountability.*
- Slows things down without improving them.
- Adds approvals that feel performative, not protective.
- Prioritizes the process over the outcome.
- Discourages adaptation with phrases like, "That's just how we do it."

Honestly, you can usually *feel* the difference even if you can't articulate it. Supportive systems feel like a net. Bureaucratic ones feel like a trap.

Here's a quick test. Ask yourself: Does this thing we do exist to create clarity, quality, or coherence? Or does it exist because it's always existed, or because it's "just easier"? The key in that sentence is that the word "just" is doing a lot of work.

Think about it this way: Have you ever resisted training that person on tasks you know should be delegated because you rationalize to yourself that "It's just easier if I do it myself"? Yeah, that.

If your answer lives in the first bucket, that's Valuable Friction. If it lives in any of the second, it's probably time to remove—or reframe—that part of your process.

Three Tools that Make Friction Feel Supportive

Every team, household, or solo operation has a rhythm. The question is: *does it serve you or just reflect the chaos around you?*

When friction is designed with care, rhythm becomes a strategic asset. And three of the most powerful tools for creating healthy operational friction are rhythm, ritual, and review.

Rhythm: Make the Pace Predictable

A steady rhythm reduces anxiety. It turns urgency into tempo.

- Weekly check-ins to align on what matters *now*
- Monthly retros to surface what's working (and what's wearing thin)
- Quarterly planning that focuses attention—and fends off scope creep

Rhythm doesn't have to mean rigidity. It means your system has a pulse—so people aren't left guessing where to put their energy.

Ritual: Build In Meaningful Pause

This one is my favorite. Rituals are intentional pauses that reconnect us to what matters.

- A one-word check-in to start team meetings
- Five minutes of silence before strategic discussions
- A family "rose and thorn" dinner conversation to reflect on the day
- A content rule: *every piece gets reviewed by someone outside the project*

The best rituals are lightly sacred. They introduce just enough friction to create presence—without killing momentum.

Review: Reflect Before You Repeat

Reviews aren't just for reporting. They're a chance to recalibrate.

- What did we set out to do?
- What surprised us?
- What's worth carrying forward or leaving behind?

Done well, reviews turn motion into progress. They protect the system from decay and the people from burnout. They make sure success wasn't just a fluke—and that failure isn't wasted.

Operational Friction is...the Difference

It's easy to think of operations—our process—as backstage work: necessary but invisible. But the way we operate doesn't just shape how we function. It shapes how we *show up*—for our family, our colleagues, our customers. It's not separate from how we're perceived. It *becomes* how we're perceived.

In the end, standing out isn't about having a louder message or a flashier presence. It's about having a rhythm. A stance. A way of moving that is unmistakably yours.

Anyone can deliver once. Anyone can look polished for a season. But operational friction builds muscle. It's what makes distinctiveness sustainable. Those thoughtfully designed systems, rituals, and rhythms don't just support the work—they *train* us to show up again and again with clarity, intention, and integrity.

- A founder who protects their priorities through well-drawn constraints builds a business that reflects their values—not just the market's noise.
- A team with a thoughtful cadence and clear rituals builds a culture others want to work with and work for.
- A family with shared practices and boundaries creates a kind of presence that feels grounded—even in chaos.
- A student with a working architecture for decision making moves through uncertainty with surprising coherence.

This is what friction enables: not just progress but *strength in motion*. The kind of strength that can adapt without breaking. Persist without losing shape. Recover without losing rhythm.

And that's the part no one can copy: the lived-in structure that makes your work *yours*.

The best systems don't just help us move forward. They help us move forward *as ourselves*—with the muscle to keep going and the memory to do it well.

CHAPTER 8

Relational Friction

Slow Conversations that Outlast any Scroll

"Try to see it my way
Only time will tell if I am right or I am wrong
While you see it your way
There's a chance that we might fall apart before too long
We can work it out
We can work it out"

—The Beatles, "We Can Work It Out"

This might be the hardest part of the book. Not because the ideas are more complex, but because the terrain is so personal. Relationships—whether professional or personal—are where the stakes are highest. And over the last 25 years, they're also where we've seen some of the deepest erosion.

We've gotten used to disconnection in slow motion. Technology promised closeness but delivered convenience. We can react instantly but rarely respond well. We have tools to "stay in touch," but no time to stay in sync.

The problem isn't just pace. It's the *distortion* of pace.

We've built systems—scrolling feeds, voice notes, Slack messages, DMs, fast-twitch reaction cycles—that optimize for immediacy. And in doing so, we've sped past something essential. These systems reward performance over presence. Surface over depth. Judgment over curiosity.

Relational Friction is what helps us resist that drift. It's the pull of the heart—the steady, sometimes uncomfortable beat that reminds us to slow down, to tune in, to care enough to sit with tension rather than bypass it.

We don't lose relationships all at once. We lose them in a thousand tiny moments of missed rhythm.

But with friction—the right kind—we can start to find the beat again.

To demonstrate, let me bring you into my little movie.

It's 7:05 p.m. on a Tuesday. We open on a family kitchen.

Carla, who thinks in bullet points and talks in rapid-fire bursts, is plating tacos for her family. Across the table, her partner Luis is still turning over the day's events at work in his head—he won't know what he thinks until he's written it in his notebook later tonight. Their nine-year-old wants an answer now about a weekend trip. Carla launches into pros and cons; Luis asks for a moment; the child is already Googling ticket prices.

Five minutes of mild chaos later, nobody's furious—but nobody's inspired either. All the raw material for a great decision (speed, reflection, fresh data) sat right there on the table, spinning out of sync. The trip may or may not happen. Luis may have captured his thoughts well. The tacos were wolfed down and no one ever thanked Carla for making them.

What they lacked wasn't trust. It was rhythm.

We pull back from the kitchen—and slowly dissolve to a crowded WeWork office space.
It's 9:17 a.m. on a Wednesday.

Ari, a solo founder with three browser windows and twelve Slack channels open, is firing off a quick voice note to the company's designer. Mid-sentence, a client pings with an "urgent" change to tomorrow's pitch. Ari toggles tabs, rewrites the deck title, glances at a calendar, and realizes a product sprint kickoff is starting in four minutes.

Across the screen, the part-time CTO is typing slowly, methodically thinking through a product trade-off to bring up at the kickoff, one paragraph at a time. Meanwhile, the growth consultant has already shipped a hot take into the shared doc with bold red copy and the comment: "We just need to move."

No one's wrong. But no one's aligned either.

Three different speeds. Three different definitions of "ready." A flurry of action—but little resonance.

The trust is there. The urgency is there. But the rhythm is missing.

The camera pulls back and the scene dissolves into a marketing manager staring at a Zoom call on a screen.
It's 3:42 p.m. on a Thursday.

The marketing lead, Jordan, is briskly walking through the new campaign draft by screen-sharing a presentation with bullets, metrics, and rollout timeline. Maya, the content strategist, is worried that the message is drifting and wants to slow down to revisit the positioning. Dev, the marketing analyst, quietly flags a Slack message: early data says email open rates are dipping fast.

Nobody disagrees. But no one pauses either.

Jordan's moving fast because leadership needs a deck by morning. Maya's gut is churning from the tension—is it worth raising the positioning again? Dev's waiting to be asked. Everyone's trying to be efficient—and no one's being heard.

The collaboration is there. The intent is good. But the rhythm is off.

Fade out…

That restless space where people's tempos, viewpoints, and comfort zones don't quite line up—that's Relational Friction. Managed well, it becomes the spark that turns familiar voices into unexpected wisdom. Managed poorly, it's just awkward and unproductive.

Why this Isn't Another "Trust Fall" Manual

Most relationship advice aims to smooth out the bumps. Increase transparency. Flatten hierarchy. Align everything. Make everyone comfortable.

That's not what this motion is about.

Relational Friction argues almost the opposite: keep the bumps, but design the pauses. Build guardrails. Create enough structure that differences don't get paved over and enough time that disagreement can ripen into insight.

It's not about being in sync all the time. It's about learning to metabolize the moments when we're *not*. Because when we move too fast to notice our differences, we don't just miss opportunities—we miss each other.

Let's begin.

When Smooth becomes Shallow

I don't think it's too dramatic to say that we've witnessed an unraveling of relationships over the last 25 years—one that didn't happen all at once but steadily deepened across every layer of modern life.

Study after study points to declining trust in institutions, neighbors, even close friends. According to Pew Research, the percentage of Americans who say most people can be trusted has dropped significantly since the late 1990s.[20] The NORC General Social Survey has tracked a steep decline in the number of people who say they have close confidants.[21] Meanwhile, political polarization has reached record highs, with social media amplifying ideological silos and rewarding outrage over dialogue. Dating apps and algorithmic matchmaking have reshaped intimacy into a marketplace of constant comparison, while friendship itself has become more fragmented—

especially for men and young adults, whose reported levels of loneliness have climbed dramatically in the last decade.[22]

It's not just that we're spending less time with one another; it's that we're spending that time through systems that weren't designed for depth. What we're seeing isn't the end of connection but the erosion of the rhythms that sustain it.

This unraveling of relationships didn't happen in a dramatic moment. It's been subtle. Gradual. The kind of drift that's easy to miss in real time.

At a personal level, it begins when we start to skip the small pauses—the moment before we respond, the extra beat it takes to ask a real question instead of making a fast judgment, the quiet space between what someone *says* and what they *mean*. We tell ourselves we're being efficient. We assume everyone's on the same page. We feel productive, in rhythm, forward-moving.

But what we've really done is start replacing relationship time with reaction time.

It's not that we've stopped caring about one another. It's that our systems—our tools, our habits, our schedules—have made it harder to *show* that we care in any meaningful way. Technology didn't cause that shift entirely, but it has certainly accelerated it. When we start referring to every conversation as a ping, a thread, a check-in squeezed between other tasks, we begin to relate in shorthand. We value headline over nuance, alignment over difference, ease over depth.

And we do this with the best of intentions. We're trying to avoid conflict. We're trying to be respectful of time. We're trying to keep things moving. But in doing so, we smooth over the very things that make a relationship feel alive—difference, surprise, perspective, and the occasional discomfort of not being fully in sync.

Over time, this kind of smoothing has consequences. It becomes harder to say something that might take a few minutes to explain. Harder to hear something that wasn't said with perfect tone. Harder to recover from a misstep when there's no room built in to step back.

And without realizing it, we start holding each other at a polite distance—not out of malice, but because the tempo just doesn't leave room for the messier, slower parts of being connected.

In other words (and pay attention, because here comes that word again): it's just easier not to engage. Easier to scroll past, to say nothing, to stay in your lane—because there's less risk of confrontation, less risk of getting it wrong, less risk of that deeply modern discomfort: being perceived as "cringe" or being "cancelled".

Ease, in this context, isn't neutral. It's shaping our relationships by quietly editing out everything that takes time, care, or courage.

The cost isn't just emotional—it's creative, cultural, strategic. Teams that move too fast to tolerate disagreement make safer choices. Families that operate like project boards miss the chance for spontaneous connection. Even long-standing partnerships can become transactional when everything is measured in immediate response.

We don't fall apart all at once. We fall apart by forgetting to make space for one another's timing. One skipped pause at a time.

Relational Friction begins to change that—not by insisting we slow everything down, but by inviting us to be just a little more intentional with how we handle the differences we already live with. It gives us a way to sit in those small misalignments, not as failures to be corrected but as invitations to learn each other's rhythms again.

Not everything needs to be easy. Some of the most meaningful things in life never are.

What Friction Makes Possible

For something that often feels awkward in the moment, Relational Friction turns out to be quietly essential—not just for connection, but for creativity, resilience, and growth.

When you think about the best conversations you've ever had—the ones that lingered in your mind for days afterward—they probably weren't smooth. They likely involved some discomfort. A pause. A moment of vulnerability. A shift in tempo or tone that forced you to pay closer attention. That's friction doing its work.

When it's unstructured, friction can feel chaotic. But when it's shaped with care—when we build in space for difference, disagreement, or simply a slower rhythm—it becomes the condition for depth.

- It lets teams stop operating on default mode and start surfacing real insight.
- It lets families pause long enough to hear each other beneath the noise.
- It lets friendships stretch without snapping.
- It lets partnerships evolve instead of calcifying around convenience.

And it does something else, too: it brings forward voices that would otherwise go unheard.

In the workplace, it's easy to over-rely on the fast responders, the loudest contributors, the ones who thrive in real-time discussion. But research shows that many of the strongest ideas don't come from the fastest thinkers—they come from the slow metabolizers. The people who sit with the question a little longer. Who revise. Who reflect.

Structured relational friction creates space for those voices to emerge. Not just by telling people to "speak up," but by shifting the rhythm so the room can actually hear them when they do.

It also builds trust—not through artificial transparency or oversharing, but through earned understanding. When you let someone move at their own tempo, or disagree without consequence, or contribute in their own voice and not the expected tone, you send a signal: *You belong here, just as you are*. That kind of trust doesn't need to be constantly stated. You can feel it in the space between words.

Perhaps most importantly, Relational Friction makes relationships more durable.

Not every disagreement needs to be solved immediately. Not every hard moment needs a script. Sometimes what's needed most is the pause. The space. The ability to stay present when it's tempting to smooth things over.

Relational Friction doesn't always feel comfortable. But it does help us stay—through the awkwardness, the mismatch, the misfires—long enough to find something real on the other side.

How to Practice Relational Friction

The kind of friction that strengthens relationships doesn't happen by accident. It has to be designed—gently, intentionally, and in ways that feel natural to the people involved. Not every group needs the same structure, but every group benefits from some.

Honestly—this topic could be an entire book and, while I'll provide some guidelines here, I can only scratch the surface.

I find Relational Friction has three core ingredients. Think of them as principles you can adapt to your context, whether you're leading a team, raising kids, or trying to collaborate across personalities and paces.

1. Rhythmic Dissonance—Honoring different Personal Tempos

Not everyone thinks, speaks, or decides at the same speed. In most modern settings—especially workplaces—we unconsciously reward speed. Quick responses, fast meetings, fast pivots, instant feedback. But quick isn't always wise. And over time, it narrows the space for certain kinds of contributions. We often chalk it up to the format (e.g. "you can't understand tone in a text message"), or even more recently even punctuation (some younger people now see periods at the end of sentences as denoting aggression). But those are symptoms of the broader issue—which is that speed has replaced care in how re communicate.

Relational Friction invites a different approach. It says to let people move at their own rhythm and build in enough room that those rhythms don't cancel each other out.

In Practice:

- Replace "respond in real time" with "respond by end of day" when soliciting feedback.
- Allow asynchronous contributions in brainstorms and decision-making processes.
- At home, check in after the meeting or dinner—some people formulate their thoughts later, not during.

A moment of silence in a conversation might not be a lull. It might be where the real insight is starting to form.

Here's a delightfully awkward experiment: lace deliberate silence into your next brainstorm. About 30 minutes in, announce, "We're taking a seven-minute quiet break—yes, seven, not five." The oddball number jolts people out of autopilot, just like starting a meeting at 8:12 or 12:34 makes calendars double-take. Tiny friction, sharper focus.

Drop two more seven-minute pauses into a 90-minute session. After the third round, pair everyone up for ten minutes toward the end to trade their biggest *aha*. Each duo surfaces one takeaway for the whole group while keeping any half-baked or personal reflections private. The result? You get richer ideas (because introverts finally have runway), a tighter shared understanding (because insights are distilled before they go public), and a room that learns to value thinking time as much as talking time.

2. Perspective Collision—Curating Voices that Will (Productively) Disagree

Healthy friction often starts with difference. But difference without structure can feel random or hostile. The goal isn't to fight—it's to *design for creative abrasion*; to invite people in who will challenge the dominant view and then make it safe to stay in the discomfort long enough to find something better.

In Practice:

- Assign a "devil's advocate" in team discussions—not to derail the plan, but to stretch the thinking.
- Invite someone from outside the project (or department) to review a piece of work and ask them: "What's not landing for you?"
- In families, ask: "What's something we might be missing?" before finalizing a big decision.

The point isn't constant tension. It's enough structured tension to reveal blind spots, open perspective, and deepen collective intelligence.

3. Structured Pause—Embedding Slow Loops that Metabolize Tension

Most teams (and families) are good at moving forward. Few are good at slowing down just long enough to reflect. But reflection is where relationships stabilize. It's where we name misalignments before they harden, revisit hard moments before they calcify, and give people room to breathe. Structured pauses aren't indulgences—they're maintenance…even if not everyone loves the tune-up.

If a teammate grumbles ("Can't we just get on with it?"), honor the impatience first: *"I know this feels slow when we're revved up."* Then reframe the pause as an efficiency play, not a speed bump: one silent minute now can save a 30-minute post-mortem later. Invite skeptics to track their own "aha" moments over a few meetings; their tally usually converts them faster than any pep talk.

In Practice:

- **End meetings with one minute of silence**, then ask: "Is there anything we haven't said?" and make it okay for the answer to be "Nope, all good."
- **Build "cool-down" space into tough conversations**: pause, stretch, grab coffee, come back. Let opt-outs listen quietly if talking feels forced.
- **Set rituals for reflection**: weekly check-ins, quarterly family debriefs, annual retreat dinners where the goal is not to solve but to listen.

These pauses protect the relationship by surfacing what doesn't always appear in real time. They turn unspoken tension into understood truth.

Relational Friction doesn't require formal systems or forced vulnerability. It just asks us to resist the urge to smooth everything over—adding a little structure, a touch of delay, a pinch of dissonance—so everyone can stay fully themselves while still finding a shared way forward.

Build Staying Power with Structure

I've been married for 33 years, and that's not because my wife and I have agreed on everything (if that were the standard, we'd have lasted about three weeks). It's not the absence of friction that's kept us strong—it's the ability to hold it, to move through misalignment without rushing past it or shutting it down. To stay present in the in-between spaces, even when those spaces are uncomfortable, slow, or unresolved.

Relational Friction is what makes that kind of staying possible.

It's easy to assume that relationships thrive when everything feels aligned.

But relationships are rarely (or never) smooth all the time. We are all human, after all. So, more often, what makes a relationship meaningful isn't the ease—it's how we relate when it's *not* easy. When the rhythms don't match. When one person wants to move and the other needs a minute. When the answers don't come right away, or come out wrong, or come with edges that need to be softened over time.

Relational Friction is what gives those moments structure. Not to fix them, but to allow for the natural misalignments of real human interaction—and to trust that something worthwhile can still emerge.

Because the truth is, most people don't remember you for how smooth you were. They remember how you made them feel when things weren't smooth. When the pace was off, the question was hard, or the conversation turned but you didn't turn away.

This is how we stand out—not by being frictionless but by building the kind of presence that knows how to stay in the room when things get uncertain.

It's not always graceful. But it's often where grace begins.

CHAPTER 9

The Practice of Friction

Turning Theory into Muscle Memory,
One Intention at a Time

> *"You can choose a ready guide in some celestial voice*
> *If you choose not to decide, you still have made a choice,*
> *You can choose from phantom fears, and kindness that can kill*
> *I will choose a path that's clear, I will choose free will."*
>
> —Rush, "Freewill"

There are four motions in this book exploring what I call the Four Forms of Valuable Friction—creative, strategic, operational, and relational. Each lives where you actually have agency: how you create, decide, operate, and relate. Outside forces matter—markets, algorithms, luck—but the friction that shapes meaning starts on the inside.

These aren't just abstract ideas. They're capacities. Practices. And together, they form something like a whole-body system for moving through the world with intention.

- **Creative Friction** activates the mind—sharpening thought and shaping originality.

- **Strategic Friction** engages the gut—giving you the pause and inner clarity to choose direction wisely.
- **Operational Friction** builds muscle—through repeatable, embodied structure and rhythm.
- **Relational Friction** opens the heart—making space for real connection, even when it's uncomfortable.

You don't need all four at full strength all the time. But when they move in concert—when mind, gut, muscle, and heart are aligned—you don't just work more effectively. You show up more fully.

These are not the only four areas of your life worth examining, but I've chosen to focus on them for a reason. They offer a useful frame. A grounded place to begin. For me, they've become the lens that helps me stand apart and differentiate myself—which, if we're honest, is part of what this book is about.

But wait—stand out? Differentiate? Why is that so important? Isn't that just the obsession of marketers and companies?

Not really. Not if you look deeper.

Standing out isn't about being flashy. It's about being rooted. It's about moving in a way that is unmistakably yours. And these four forms of friction? They're how you build the kind of presence that doesn't just attract attention—but holds meaning.

Before we begin this motion, let's pause for a moment and pressure test something.

Why Stand Out?

"Standing out" isn't a vanity flex; it's a civic, psychological, and spiritual imperative. Valuable Friction is the gym equipment that strengthens those muscles.

Consider Danish theologian and philosopher Søren Kierkegaard, who urged us to live "inwardly"[23] as an act of rebellion against the easy drag of the crowd. Truth, for him, isn't a prefab kit we inherit; it's a choice we wrestle into being. Authentic life starts when we stop outsourcing convictions to public opinion and instead examine the anxious pause between stimulus and response.

Psychology backs this up. Self-Determination Theory shows autonomy is essential for flourishing, while Cal Newport's *Deep Work* warns that algorithmic sameness sandpapers that autonomy away.[24]

And as Nassim Taleb reminds us in his book *Antifragile*, what can't be distinguished becomes fragile—commoditized, replaceable, ready for the next bit of code to swallow. Differentiation is anti-fragility in action, a buffer against being flattened by speed culture.[25]

Put ever so simply: If you color yourself the exact same shade as everyone else, nobody (including you) can tell which crayon you are. Keep your colors bright because the whole picture needs you.

The Practice of Friction

How do we keep our edges sharp without turning life into a nonstop branding exercise? We practice. Just as a musician runs scales or an athlete drills footwork, we cultivate small, intentional moments of Valuable Friction—choices that slow us down, thicken our presence, and carve out shape.

Valuable Friction as a differentiating motion is simply a habit to inhabit: a daily discipline of resisting the easy glide path so the contours of who you are—parent, student, entrepreneur, citizen—can emerge in high relief.

It's important to remember that not all friction is valuable. Some of it really is just sludge—confusing forms, clunky workflows, needless delays, bad habits that calcified into process. And to be clear: that kind of friction should go.

But when we adopt a blanket mindset of "friction = bad," we risk throwing out the very things that make our work deeper, our systems more resilient, and our relationships more real.

So how do we tell the difference?

It starts with a shift in posture, from minimizing friction to interrogating it. Before we cut, we pause. Before we streamline, we study. We ask: *What kind of resistance is this? What purpose does it serve? What might we lose if it disappears?*

Here's a simple starting point: Sludge slows without serving while friction slows to signal, shape, or strengthen. I'll list some key signs illustrating the difference:

Friction worth preserving (or designing):

- Invites reflection, not just reaction
- Builds trust (through clarity, transparency, or participation)
- Signals that something matters (e.g., confirmation steps in a user interface, slow reveals)
- Anchors the perception of quality or craftsmanship—like the way Apple products all have a similar and slightly friction-filled way of unboxing
- Gives a sense of ritual, care, or personal investment
- Acts as a useful boundary, constraint, or filter

Friction worth eliminating (or redesigning):

- Confuses ownership or accountability
- Causes people to disengage without understanding why
- Delays without adding meaning or insight
- Exists purely out of habit, not intention

- Creates fear, shame, or unnecessary complexity
- Is invisible or arbitrary to the person experiencing it

The trick isn't to optimize for ease. It's to optimize for integrity. For clarity. For connection. For trust. Which means we don't always ask, *"How can we make this faster?"* Sometimes we ask, *"Where might a little resistance help us get this just right?"* That's the heart of the practice—turning down the reflex to remove resistance and turning up the curiosity to understand it.

How to Audit Your Systems, Decisions, and Experiences through a Friction Lens

If friction is a signal, then your work, systems, and relationships are full of signals just waiting to be noticed.

But you can't work with what you can't see. And most friction—good or bad—is easy to overlook, because we've either normalized or eliminated it by default. So the first step in building a friction practice is making friction visible.

This is where a friction audit comes in. Think of it as a guided scan across your work, your team, or your day to identify where resistance exists, how it manifests itself, and how it's shaping outcomes.

You can apply this audit to:

- A workflow or process (e.g., onboarding, content review, meetings)
- A product or experience (e.g., how someone buys, subscribes, learns, or engages)
- A team ritual (e.g., how decisions are made or feedback is shared)
- A personal habit (e.g., how you start your day, structure creative time, or avoid difficult conversations)

The goal isn't to judge. It's to notice.

Try asking:

1. **Where is there friction?**

   What feels slow, awkward, effortful, or uncertain?

2. **Is the friction visible or invisible?**

   Is it something people recognize or something they've stopped noticing?

3. **What kind of friction is it?**

   Is it creative (tension that could spark or stifle originality)? Strategic (a pause in decision-making)? Operational (challenging a structure)? Relational (an unspoken tension)?

4. **What is it doing?**

   Is it creating focus, prompting clarity, or slowing things down in a healthy way?

   Or is it wasting time, draining energy, or eroding trust?

5. **What happens if we remove it or design it better?**

   Would we lose something meaningful? Or gain something valuable?

This kind of audit doesn't require a spreadsheet. It requires a lens.

It's a way of seeing friction as information, not just interference. As a design material. As a storytelling device. As a trust-building behavior. As a clue.

For Creators—Making Things that are More than Just Content

In a world optimized for output, speed, and virality, choosing to make something *with care*—and to ask something of your audience in return—is a radical move.

This is where friction becomes not just a design principle but a creative ethic.

As a creator—whether you write, record, design, teach, code, perform, or curate—you're under constant pressure to make things easier. Easier to consume. Easier to share. Easier to forget.

But the work that lasts—the work that resonates and connects with an audience—usually asks for a little more.

A little more attention.

A little more craft.

A little more *you*.

From a creative content or product design, this friction is when you choose not to smooth everything down. When you let the process stay a little difficult and invite your audience to participate in that difficulty too.

This might mean:

- Choosing a format that requires reflection instead of endless scrolling
- Creating a narrative arc that rewards patience, not just punchlines
- Saying something that risks being misunderstood but is worth the risk (like a form field on your email subscriber page that asks what their favorite food is)
- Releasing less content, but making more of what you release

Friction doesn't mean being obscure. It means being *intentional* about what you make easy and what you make meaningful.

Because what your audience remembers is not just what was fast, clever, or clickable. It's what made them feel something. It's what made them work just enough to remember that *they* were part of the process, too.

And when you, as the creator, build an experience with a little tension, a little care, a little pause—you don't just make content.

You make connection.

For Leaders—Creating Valuable Friction in a World of Asymmetry

Leadership isn't just a matter of decision-making. It's a matter of *designing how clarity happens in environments full of asymmetry*—asymmetry of information and asymmetry of relationships.

You often know more than your team does about priorities, pressures, and internal politics. You also often feel less of the interpersonal risk. People hesitate to push back, to ask questions, to offer truth. That's the nature of hierarchy, even in flat systems.

This means that friction becomes your job. Not to eliminate it, but to create the conditions where it becomes useful, visible, and safe.

Valuable Friction in leadership isn't about slowing your team down. It's about helping them move through confusion with structure, not assumptions. It's the friction that says:

- "Let's sit with that trade-off a little longer."
- "Let's make the disagreement useful, not silent."
- "Let's not conflate consensus with clarity."

As a leader, you must constantly design for symmetry—not by leveling all information or relationships but by building spaces where challenge can surface without punishment. Where tension becomes a source of alignment rather than erosion.

That might look like:

- A decision-making process that separates fast action from long-term bets
- Structured feedback channels that go in *both* directions
- Norms that distinguish disagreement from disloyalty

- Planning rituals that include second-order thinking (e.g., "What are we not seeing?")

The irony is that people don't trust leaders who move too fast to be questioned. They trust leaders who invite productive hesitation—who hold the tension just long enough for something better to emerge.

In a world where power often moves faster than perspective, friction is what keeps leadership human. It's the pause that restores trust. The structure that creates courage. The breath between "yes" and "why".

Friction isn't a failure of leadership. It's a form of presence and cultivating relationships.

For teams—Creating Rhythms and Rituals that Support Both Speed and Sanity

Teams don't fall apart because they don't care. They fall apart because they move faster than their trust can keep up. They misalign. They misread. They move on without saying what needed to be said. And then they wake up one morning running the same processes—but with half the energy and none of the shared meaning.

That's where Operational and Relational Friction come in—not as blockers, but as anchors.

Because healthy teams don't just need clarity. They need *cadence*. A rhythm that holds them steady. A pattern that creates shared understanding without requiring constant checking in or re-deciding. A structure that slows things down just enough to make sure they're moving *together*—not just moving at the same time.

Friction helps that happen in ways that look deceptively small.

For example:

- A weekly meeting that starts with one minute of silence—because quiet minds make better plans.

- A shared doc where everyone adds one "risk no one's talking about."
- A norm that says, "We don't finalize until someone says what they're unsure about."
- A meeting format that includes relationship and collaboration check-ins—not just tasks and blockers.

Rituals like these introduce friction through repetition and pause. They may not feel efficient, but they make things *coherent*. And over time, they build the connective tissue that makes speed sustainable.

Real team alignment isn't about agreement—it's about shared commitment. And commitment is built not in the rush but in the rhythm.

When teams embed friction into their systems—not just their culture slides—they stop having to scramble for trust. They *earn* it. They *practice* it. They reinforce it in the ordinary.

For Marketers and Communicators—Designing Memorable Experiences

In marketing, the default setting is ease: reduce clicks, shorten funnels, automate follow-ups, and make everything simple, fast, and seamless.

And, to be fair, there's a place for that. Nobody wants to fight a checkout page or fill out a 12-step form. But if everything is too easy, too smooth, too instantaneous, nothing stands out. Frictionless is forgettable.

This is why friction, when used with intention, becomes not just a differentiator but a storyteller. A memory-maker. A trust builder.

As a marketer or communicator, friction is one of the most underused tools you have to create resonance.

- It's the extra second that builds anticipation.
- The interaction that requires someone to choose.

- The narrative that unfolds slowly enough to be felt—not just scanned.
- The call to action that makes someone pause—*not because it's unclear, but because it's worth considering.*

Strategic and Creative Friction intersect here. You're not just optimizing an experience. You're shaping meaning.

That might mean:

- A form that asks one unexpected, personal question
- A confirmation step that frames the *why* behind the request
- A storytelling arc that doesn't front load everything in the first two lines
- A visual or audio cue that takes just a beat longer than expected
- A reward that's tied to the user doing something active—not just clicking

Friction in marketing isn't about slowing conversion. It's about creating emotional investment.

It's what turns a product into a ritual. A message into a memory. A click into a choice.

And it's how, in a landscape ruled by convenience, you can still create something that's not just consumed but considered.

For Educators—Helping Learners Engage with the Struggle, not Escape It

Education is often mistaken for information transfer. But real learning doesn't happen when something is simply explained. It happens when it's *wrestled with*. When it's felt. When a learner is asked to stay with the difficulty just long enough to grow through it.

That's where Valuable Friction in education lives—not in confusion for its own sake but in thoughtfully placed resistance that turns passive exposure into active engagement.

As an educator—whether in a classroom, workshop, training, or coaching environment—your job isn't to eliminate friction. It's to *design it*. To create the kinds of obstacles that sharpen attention, provoke curiosity, and build confidence—not crush it.

That might look like:

- Asking a student to attempt an answer before teaching the concept
- Withholding the "right answer" until the process has been explored
- Giving formative feedback that challenges without overwhelming
- Creating projects with real-world ambiguity, not binary outcomes
- Designing group work where interpersonal tension becomes part of the learning

These aren't hurdles. They're invitations. They say: *This matters enough to not come easily.*

Psychologists call this kind of challenge a desirable difficulty—friction that strengthens long-term retention, problem solving, and self-awareness. But to use it well, you need emotional scaffolding: clear expectations, safety to fail, and support when the friction gets frustrating.

When you give learners too little resistance, they coast. But when you give them the right kind, in the right moment, they *build something inside themselves.*

That's not just education. That's transformation.

For Anyone—Living with Less Rush and More Return

You don't have to be a leader, an educator, or a creator to work with friction.

You just have to be someone who's tired of everything needing to be faster.

Someone who's noticed that even your weekends feel optimized. That your phone wants you to scroll, your calendar wants you to rush, and your brain rarely gets to rest.

And the question it asks is simple: What would it look like to build a life that included a little more friction—on purpose?

That might mean:

- Making space for slowness—walking instead of driving, reading instead of skimming
- Reclaiming rituals—cooking from scratch, writing by hand, pausing before you post
- Creating separation—turning off notifications, building white space into your day
- Practicing presence—doing one thing at a time and letting it be enough

Friction, in daily life, doesn't have to be profound. It just has to be *real*.

It's the pause before the reaction. The breath before the reply. The moment where you choose depth over default, again and again.

Because the point of this book isn't just better ideas or stronger teams. It's a life that feels less like a race and more like a rhythm. Less about control and more about *care*.

That's the promise of friction as a practice. Not to make life harder—but to make it matter more.

From Awareness to Action: Your Friction Diagnostic

You've now seen how Valuable Friction can help you create better ideas, make better decisions, build better systems, strengthen relationships, and craft more memorable experiences. In addition to being summarized in this chapter, each of the four is examined in more depth in its own chapter.

But knowing *about* the Four Forms isn't the same as *applying* them.

That's why I've created a simple companion diagnostic—a set of tools and prompts to help you work through friction in your own life, work, team, or organization. It's designed to help you spot opportunities, name patterns, and begin shaping your own friction practice with clarity and care.

The diagnostic contains:

- A guided friction audit you can apply to a process, a relationship, or a project
- Quick diagnostic questions for each of the Four Forms
- A worksheet to map where friction is serving you—and where it's silently stalling you
- Prompts to spark conversation with your team, collaborators, or clients

These are not tests—and they're not templates. They are simply mirrors. A tool to help you notice what's already there—and decide, with more wisdom, what to preserve, what to remove, and what to redesign with more intention.

You can find the full diagnostic and reflection kit in the downloadable companion to this book [or at: www.valuablefriction.com].

Because, like any good practice, this isn't just something you *know*. It's something you *live into*—over time.

CHAPTER 10

The Fewer-Better-Bolder Manifesto

Standing Apart by Choosing Less, Deciding Better, and Acting Louder

> *"Look out kid*
> *It's somethin' you did*
> *God knows when*
> *But you're doin' it again*
> *You better duck down the alley way*
> *Lookin' for a new friend*
> *The man in the coon-skin cap*
> *By the big pen*
> *Wants eleven dollar bills*
> *You only got ten"*
>
> —Bob Dylan, *"Subterranean Homesick Blues"*

You are either beginning, continuing, or finishing a book about friction—a small book that asks you to slow down, pay attention, and wrestle with the moments that don't move quickly or easily.

So it's fitting that this book closes not with a summary but with a stance. A manifesto. A set of convictions that remind us of what we're choosing when we choose friction—not as a burden, but as a design for depth.

Because friction isn't just a creative constraint or a process checkpoint. It's not just a moment of hesitation or a tough conversation. It's a whole-body rhythm. A way of moving through life with the mind engaged, the heart open, the gut grounded, and the muscle steady.

Each form of Valuable Friction lives in a part of us:

- The **mind** sharpens through creative tension—wrestling with ideas until they take shape.
- The **gut** speaks in strategic pauses—quiet clarity before the leap.
- The **muscle** is built through operational rhythm—reps, rituals, and resilience.
- And the **heart** opens through relational honesty—where discomfort gives birth to trust.

You don't need all of them at once. But when they move together—when you're thinking with focus, deciding with clarity, working with rhythm, and connecting with care—something more integrated emerges. Something wiser. Something unmistakably *you*.

Before we distill, let's wrestle just a bit more.

Friction isn't just a creative constraint or a process checkpoint—it's a civilizational rhythm. It's the force that arises between layers moving at different speeds, asking us to pay attention, to adapt, to evolve. As Stewart Brand suggested in his Pace Layering model: fast layers innovate, slow layers stabilize. But it's the tension between them—the Valuable Friction—that keeps the whole system from flying apart.

This is our opportunity to step back and see friction not just as a productivity principle but as part of nature's pattern language. A form of wisdom hidden in plain sight.

Because if we rush to eliminate friction in the name of convenience or optimization, we risk dissolving the connective tissue that binds ideas, people, and purpose. In a world obsessed with acceleration, the ability to embrace and design for the right kind of resistance may be one of the most important skills we have.

This is not a checklist. It's a compass.

A way of orienting your work, your choices, your relationships, and your presence around what actually holds up. What actually matters.

This motion isn't about slowing down for its own sake.

It's about moving through the world while embracing fewer, better, bolder:

- Fewer things, chosen with care.
- Better decisions, because they're made with clarity, not panic.
- Bolder choices, because you've done the work to trust your gut.

So, I close with a suggested meditation. A manifesto, if you prefer. A return to center.

A breath.

At some point, take a few deep breaths. Slowly. And repeat.

The Fewer-Better-Bolder Manifesto

We believe friction is not a flaw.
It's a signal. A sculptor. A source of shape.
It's what gives work its weight,
trust its teeth,
and meaning its memory.
We live in a world that worships speed, ease, and scale.
But I choose to move differently.
I choose fewer things—because we want them to matter.
I choose better decisions—not rushed but rooted.
I choose bolder actions—because depth gives me direction.

I believe that friction, held with care,
can strengthen relationships, sharpen thinking, and deepen our presence.
I don't chase struggle. But I don't fear it either.
I design for the right kind of resistance.
The kind that builds something inside us while we're building something outside us.
I make space for slowness, not as retreat—but as rhythm.
I choose structure over scramble.
Substance over noise.
Presence over polish.
Commitment over convenience.
I live and work and lead in ways that leave a mark.
Not because we always move quickly,
but because we know when to hold still
and when to push forward—with intention.
This is not a method. It's a mindset.
This is not a formula. It's a field guide.
This is not about friction for friction's sake.
It's about remembering what's worth the effort.
Fewer.
Better.
Bolder.
On purpose.

A Life Worth Wrestling With

Just a final word for this motion: I didn't write this book because I felt like I had friction figured out. I wrote it because I've spent most of my life *learning to live with it*—and, sometimes, trying to avoid it.

Like a lot of people, I came up in a world that rewarded velocity. The more I could produce, the more I was praised. The faster I moved, the more opportunities I created. I was good at adapting, good at staying ahead, good at saying yes.

But somewhere along the way, something started to feel … thin. Like I was delivering at the expected speed but drifting further from the substance that made the work mine. The things I was most proud of didn't come fast. They weren't frictionless. They were hard. They took time. They required something of me—and that's what made them *real*.

This book has been a way to name that realization. To offer a language, a framework, a practice that might help others slow down—not to fall behind, but to reconnect with what they're here to do.

If that's you—if you've ever felt like the rush is crowding out the meaning—this is my invitation:

Don't speed up. Don't scale down. Don't smooth it over.

Just stay in it.

Ask better questions.

Choose fewer things.

Move when it matters.

Be bold when it counts.

That's the kind of differentiated life I'm trying to build. The kind of differentiated work I want to keep doing. And maybe, just maybe, it's what helps me feel like I'm standing apart in a world that feels ever more like it's trying to race its way to relevance.

Yes, I think practicing Valuable Friction gives me better output—clearer ideas, smarter decisions, more original work. And yes, that's helpful in the moment. But the most important thing it enables in me is a kind of grounded confidence—not just in what I make, but in who I'm becoming.

A steadier mind. A clearer path. And the belief that what I create—and who I am—might actually make a difference.

This is how I know I'm not just moving through life….I'm becoming.

Valuable Friction References

1. "We Shape Our Tools and Thereafter Our Tools Shape Us." 2017. McLuhan Galaxy. McLuhan Galaxy. September 4. https://mcluhangalaxy.wordpress.com/2013/04/01/we-shape-our-tools-and-thereafter-our-tools-shape-us/.

2. Honore, Carl. 2008. In Praise of Slowness Challenging the Cult of Speed. Paw Prints.

3. Wu, Tim. 2018. "The Tyranny of Convenience." The New York Times, February 16. https://www.nytimes.com/2018/02/16/opinion/sunday/tyranny-convenience.html.

4. Gosline, Renée Richardson. 2022. "Why AI Customer Journeys Need More Friction." Harvard Business Review. June 9. https://hbr.org/2022/06/why-ai-customer-journeys-need-more-friction?utm_source=chatgpt.com.

5. Halperin, Shirley. 2011. "Jim Ladd, the Inspiration for Tom Petty's 'the Last DJ,' Laid off from Radio Gig." The Hollywood Reporter. October 27. https://www.hollywoodreporter.com/news/general-news/jim-ladd-tom-petty-last-dj-254148/.

6. Barden, Phil P. 2020. Decoded: The Science Behind Why We Buy. S.L.: John Wiley & Sons.

7. Michael, Ann. 2010. "Shirky at NFAIS: How Abundance Breaks Everything - the Scholarly Kitchen." The Scholarly Kitchen. March 2. https://scholarlykitchen.sspnet.org/2010/03/02/shirky-at-nfais-how-abundance-breaks-everything/.

8. Egan, Mark. 2017. Nudge: Improving Decisions About Health, Wealth and Happiness. Macat Library.

9. Johnson, Cameron. 2022. "Looking Back on the Origin of Skip Intro Five Years Later." About Netflix. March 17. https://about.netflix.com/en/news/looking-back-on-the-origin-of-skip-intro-five-years-later.

10. Morris, Wesley, Elyssa Dudley, Hans Buetow, and Sasha Weiss. 2022. "Still Processing: Do You Hit 'Skip Intro'?" The New York Times, April 21. https://www.nytimes.com/2022/04/21/podcasts/still-processing-binge-skip-intro.html?.

11. Bjork, R. A. & Bjork, E. L. 2011. Making things hard on yourself, but in a good way: Creating desirable difficulties to enhance learning. In M. A. Gernsbacher, R. W. Pew, L. M. Hough, & J. R. Pomerantz (Eds.)

12. Maxwell, John C. 2023. "People Do What People See, and People Buy into the Leader Before They Buy into the Vision." Linkedin.com. September 28. https://www.linkedin.com/posts/officialjohnmaxwell_people-do-what-people-see-and-people-buy-activity-7113259550618652672-qIDW/.

13. Brand, Stewart. 2018. "Pace Layering: How Complex Systems Learn and Keep Learning." Long Now. January 17. https://longnow.org/ideas/pace-layers/.

14. Rubin, Rick & Neil, Strauss. 2023. The Creative Act: A Way of Being. Penguin Press.

15. Schwartz, Barry. 2004. The Paradox of Choice: Why More Is Less. Harper Perennial.

16. Stokes, Patricia D. 2006. Creativity from Constraints: The Psychology of Breakthrough. Springer.

17. Chesterton, Gilbert Keith. 1911. Appreciations and Criticisms of the Works of Charles Dickens. London: J. M. DENT & SONS, Ltd. New York: E. P. DUTTON & CO.

18. Acquired. 2024. "The Mark Zuckerberg Interview." YouTube. September 18. https://www.youtube.com/watch?v=QciJ9ubeLQk.

19. Ibid.

20. Chavda, Janakee. 2025. "Americans' Trust in One Another." Pew Research Center. May 8. https://www.pewresearch.org/2025/05/08/americans-trust-in-one-another/.

21. "2020 Media Coverage Highlights." 2025. Accessed June 23. https://gss.norc.org/content/dam/gss/for-survey-participants/documents/GSS%20Media%20Booklet_2020.pdf.

22. Pendell, Ryan. 2024. "1 in 5 Employees Worldwide Feel Lonely." Gallup.com. Gallup. June 12. https://www.gallup.com/workplace/645566/employees-worldwide-feel-lonely.aspx.

23. Contributors to Wikimedia projects. 2004. "Danish Philosopher and Theologian, Precursor of Existentialism." Wikiquote.org. Wikimedia Foundation, Inc. January 2. https://en.wikiquote.org/wiki/S%C3%B8ren_Kierkegaard.

24. Newport, Cal. 2016. Deep Work. Grand Central Publishing.

25. Taleb, Nassim Nicholas. 2012. Antifragile: How to Live in a World We Don't Understand. Random House.

www.ingramcontent.com/pod-product-compliance
Lightning Source LLC
Chambersburg PA
CBHW021915180426
43198CB00035B/661